The First Lady

A Comprehensive View
of
Hillary Rodham
Clinton

by Peter and Timothy Flaherty

Vital Issues Press

Vital Issues Press
P.O. Box 53788
Lafayette, Louisiana 70505

Library of Congress Card Catalog Number 96-060584
ISBN 1-56384-119-3

Printed in the U.S.A.

Contents

Photographs follow pages 31, 59, 79, 183, and 215.

Introduction

Who Is Hillary Rodham Clinton?

When she burst upon the national scene in 1992, she became the embodiment of the modern woman, juggling marriage, motherhood, and career. There were a few bumps along the way, such as the "cookies and tea" remark and getting caught spreading rumors about George Bush. All in all, however, her ascent to the White House was a triumphant one.

Her husband, the new president, was a member of a younger generation, one that came of age after World War II. Bill Clinton even looked a bit like John Kennedy, whom he had met as a teen-ager. While Bill happily emulated the youthful JFK, Hillary sought a role model in no other First Lady.

It created a sensation. No other First Lady had been a professional in her own right. No other had sought an identity apart from her husband. She had a chance to become not just a memorable First Lady, but a historic one. No other generation had experienced such a transformation in gender roles, and for many women, Hillary's reign would institutionalize the change.

In her first days in the White House, Hillary captured the national media. They built a superwoman—wife, mother, lawyer, moral exemplar. There was even talk of Hillary succeeding her husband in office.

Of course, this new role created controversy. Hillary became a lighting rod for conservative criticism, particularly when she led the effort to overhaul the nation's health care system. But, much of the flak was successfully portrayed as confirmation that Hillary was indeed breaking new ground.

Ultimately, conservatives' fears about Hillary's influence turned out to be for naught. Following the defeat on health care, no one worried anymore about a "co-president." Hillary sought refuge in the role of Traditional First Lady, to the chagrin and surprise of many of her original boosters. But, a serious study of her life shows that such a transformation should not have been surprising at all. Both liberals and conservatives have turned out to be fundamentally mistaken about Hillary's motivation, for it is more complex, and far different, than it has been understood.

In 1996, Hillary would achieve a first as First Lady. She would be subpoenaed by a special prosecutor to answer questions before a grand jury. By this time, her disapproval rating had sunk below her approval rating—another first for a First Lady. Even worse, a majority of Americans believed that she was not telling the truth about Whitewater or Travelgate.

Where Did It Go Wrong for Hillary?

Somewhere along the way, her public persona began to change. Another side began to gradually show through.

Lauded as warm and caring, Hillary took part in a series of shady financial deals in the seventies and eighties that hurt thousands of innocent people much less affluent than herself. Some of them, like the commodities dealings, have embarrassed her, while others, like a nursing home deal in Iowa, have not come to light.

In the White House, she sought the personal ruination of a man named Billie Dale, the director of the Travel Office. Dale had voted for Clinton, but he stood in the way of the enrichment of her big-shot friends, like

Hollywood producer Harry Thomason. Dale's persecution was pursued for months and months after it served any purpose, except vengeance.

Described as smart, even brilliant, Hillary could not remember key facts and events related to Whitewater when quizzed by reporters. Heralded as a feminist and a skilled lawyer, she implied that she was Jim McDougal's innocent female victim when confronted on whether she should have recognized his scams for what they were.

Portrayed as a shrewd operator and a better politician than even her husband, Hillary led the administration over the cliff to its biggest debacle, the health care defeat.

Celebrated as an advocate of poor children and the leader of the campaign for public school reform as First Lady of Arkansas, Hillary enrolled her daughter Chelsea in an exclusive private school once in Washington.

And on and on it goes. Even in her newfound role as Traditional First Lady, another side shows through. Hillary's defense mechanisms are so hair-trigger that she dissembles even when it is not necessary. For instance, she had a collaborator named Barbara Feinman on her book *It Takes a Village*. Public figures including Ronald Reagan and Colin Powell have used collaborators, if not outright ghostwriters, who are usually acknowledged, often in small print. Feinman was reportedly distraught that her name would appear nowhere. When queried about the collaborator, Hillary falsely denied that she had one. The White House even invited reporters to examine yellow legal pads of portions of the manuscript in Hillary's handwriting.

So who is Hillary Rodham Clinton? In January 1996 *New York Times* columnist William Safire called her a "congenital liar." That explanation is too simple. In response to Safire, the president suggested through his spokesman that Safire might be entitled to a punch in the nose. But, when Clinton addressed it himself at a press conference later the same day, he didn't look an-

gry. He didn't sound particularly angry, either. The reaction provided clues to the Bill and Hillary relationship.
And, it is within that relationship that the answer to the
question resides.

One

Park Ridge

"While strolling through the second floor of our library recently, I had a marvelous idea: Why not display a large portrait of Hillary Clinton? She has put Park Ridge on the map, and we should be oh so very proud of her. Now which one of our business establishments would like to generously sponsor this project?"

The idea seemed innocent enough. It was February of 1993 and the suggestion was made by a phone caller to the Park Ridge *Times Herald*. The suburban Chicago weekly invites readers to leave messages on its answering machine. The editors then print the more interesting comments in a section called "Talk of the Town." Although a few callers voiced support for Hillary, the vast majority were negative. Many were angry. The phone rang off the hook for several weeks. The newspaper staff had never seen anything like it.

> I was hoping it was a joke, but there it was in the Park Ridge Herald Editorial section. Someone wants a portrait of Hillary Clinton in our library, and wants a corporate sponsor to pay for it. What an absolutely absurd idea. What will someone think of next—Socks a poster child for the Humane Society? How has she put "Park Ridge on the map?" Okay she's the President's wife, and that probably will never happen again, but, let's use our heads, what has SHE done? . . . Let's not, and I quote, "be oh so proud" of a woman who truly feels that stay

9

at home moms sit around, relax and bake cookies all day.

Others weren't so kind.

In response to the Hillary Clinton fan who thinks Park Ridge should have a shrine in her honor. A shrine to the nation's most prominent tax cheat? Has this fan been living in a secluded cave unaware of all the sordid facts in this woman's past history that have finally seen the light of day?

What concern for children, the unemployed, the poor? Hillary Clinton has arrived where she is because of one compass—a compass that looks out for Hillary and no one else. Concern for the sick? A woman who wants to ration the world's best health care system for all of us? Is there really a clergy person who thinks Ms. Clinton is a moral leader? Heaven help us all.

The original caller was heard from again in the 2 February 1994 issue of the paper.

I'm the caller who originally suggested just a year ago, that a photo of Hillary Clinton be displayed on a wall in our public library. I didn't realize that my suggestion would result in so many subsequent derogatory calls demeaning and insulting the lady. Can't we all be proud of this young gal who grew up in our town and made it to the top as First Lady of the land? If not a photo, what? Can't the public officials do something? I'm still waiting. Thank you.

At year-end, the paper even ran a full-page retrospective on the controversy, with comments from readers on both sides. The spread included a picture of Hillary from her high-school yearbook with the caption reading "Park Ridge's favorite daughter?" There were some calls of support for Hillary, but the overwhelming majority of calls were negative.

No large portrait of Hillary Rodham Clinton was placed in the Park Ridge library, however, or even a small one. There is only a modest display of photographs from a campaign stop with her husband at Maine South High School, from which she graduated. Of course, all political figures have detractors, even in their hometowns. But, disgraced public figures from Joseph McCarthy to Richard Nixon have been accorded various levels of civic recognition. In America, fame itself is often as significant as what one is famous for.

Hillary's defenders blamed the snub on the fact that Park Ridge, an affluent suburb near O'Hare Airport, was a place where conservative and Republican political values prevailed. Indeed, its thirty-six thousand citizens voted overwhelmingly for George Bush in the 1992 election, while reelecting Republican Congressman Henry Hyde, an anti-abortion leader in the House. This is certainly part of the explanation, but not all. There is a deeper and more complex problem in the relationship between Hillary and her hometown.

Although Hillary had not seen much of Park Ridge since she left for Wellesley College in the fall of 1965, it was still home. Unlike the families of some of the corporate executives the Rodhams had for neighbors, they did not move around the country. Hillary spent her childhood and all of her formative years in Park Ridge.

That is why her debut to the world on "60 Minutes" during the campaign in January 1992 seemed so odd to people whom she had known growing up. Along with millions of viewers who had just watched the Super Bowl, they were struck by the awkwardness of Hillary having to defend her husband's infidelities. But, they noticed something else, something to them even more surprising. She spoke in a southern drawl, rather than their customary midwestern twang!

Hillary Diane Rodham was born at the Edgewater Hospital on the north side of Chicago on 26 October 1947 to Hugh and Dorothy Rodham. Dorothy named her first and only daughter Hillary because she thought it sounded exotic and unusual, especially since it was sometimes used as a boy's name.

Hugh owned and managed his own drapery business, while Dorothy was a housewife. Like most of their neighbors, the Rodhams had a big house and a big car. Hugh's house and Cadillac were not things he had known as a youth. Instead, they were testaments to his success after rather humble beginnings. He had been born in Scranton, Pennsylvania in 1912. Scranton was populated with English emigrants who spent their lives toiling in the mills and coal mines of the area. Hugh's father, also named Hugh, worked most of his life at the Scranton Lace Works Company. In fact, he had begun working there at the age of thirteen. He was a native of England, born in 1879 in the town of Northumberland, one of eleven children. He and his wife Hannah, a native of Scranton whose parents had emigrated from Wales, had three sons. Their middle son, Hugh, Hillary's father, was able to attend Pennsylvania State University on a football scholarship, and graduated in 1935 with a degree in physical education.

Upon graduation from Penn State, Hugh worked for a short time at the same factory as his father. Dissatisfied with the long hours and low wages of Scranton, and with a college degree in hand, Hugh left Pennsylvania for New York City. Hugh had taken out a marriage license with a woman from Scranton prior to his departure, although he did not return to Scranton, but rather, ended up in Chicago. It was there that he met his future wife.

Dorothy Howell was born in Chicago's working-class South Side in June of 1919. Her father, Edwin Howell, was a fireman who traced his roots to England. Dorothy's mother was Della Murray, whose father was from Canada. Her mother was from Michigan. The family left Chicago and moved to California, where Dorothy grew up in the town of Alhambra, near Pasadena. She graduated from Alhambra High School in 1937. That same year she re-

turned to Chicago. She met Hugh Rodham while apply-
ing for a secretarial job at Columbia Lace Company,
where Hugh was employed as a curtain salesman.

Hugh joined the navy a short time after meeting
Dorothy. Due to his degree in physical education, he was
assigned as an instructor to the "Gene Tunney Program,"
a navy boot camp named after the championship boxer.
Hugh trained sailors before they headed off to war. He
and Dorothy carried on a long-distance relationship for
the next five years. When Hugh completed his service in
1942, he returned to Chicago and the two were married.
Hillary, their first child, was born five years later.

According to her mother, Hillary was a "good-natured, nice little baby" and weighed eight pounds, eight
ounces at birth. Jokingly, Dorothy has said that Hillary
was "very mature upon birth." Hugh brought his daughter back to Scranton to be christened at the Court Street
Methodist Church two months after her birth. The baby
liked being read to and was the center of attention in the
Rodham's one-bedroom Chicago apartment. Hugh, at
this time, was establishing his own drapery business. His
success in this endeavor would eventually take him and
his young family to the suburbs.

In 1950 when Hillary was three, her brother Hugh
was born, and the family moved from the city to nearby
Park Ridge. Her brother Tony was born four years later.
The fifties were a time when people in large numbers
across the country were leaving cities for the suburbs.
The Rodhams settled themselves into a big comfortable
house, a brick Georgian-style house, in the country club
section of town. Park Ridge at this time was a wonderful
place to raise a young family, as the quality of life was
high and community spirit strong. Family, religion, and
education were the cornerstones of this community spirit
that was dominated by the white middle-class aspirations
of families similar to the Rodhams. It was the perfect
picture of the suburb with its tree-lined streets, mani-
cured lawns, and a quaint downtown.

In David Halberstam's authoritative work published
by Random House, *The Fifties*, he writes of the decade.

> In that era of general goodwill and expanding
> affluence, few Americans doubted the essential
> goodness of their society. . . . Most Americans
> needed little coaching in how they wanted to live.
> They were optimistic about the future. Young men
> who had spent three or four years fighting over-
> seas were eager to get on with their lives; so too,
> were the young women who had waited for them
> at home. The post-World War II rush to have chil-
> dren would later be described as the "baby boom."
> It was a good time to be young and get on with
> family and career: prices and inflation remained
> relatively low; and nearly everyone with a decent
> job could afford a home.

Park Ridge of the 1950s was full of young families. A
sense of community pervaded young Hillary's privileged,
carefree neighborhood. Dorothy Rodham told Martha
Sherrill of the *Washington Post*, "There must have been
forty or fifty children within a four block radius of our
house, and within four years of Hillary's age. They were
all together, all the time, a big extended family, there
were more boys than girls, lots of playing and competition. She held her own at cops and robbers, hide and
seek, chase and run—all games that children don't play
anymore."

Hugh was a staunch Republican and a hard worker
dedicated to his business and providing for his family.
His drapery business catered to hotels, corporations, and
airlines. In an interview with *Family Circle*, Hillary Rodham
Clinton explains, "I used to go to my father and say:
'Dad, I really need a new pair of shoes. My shoes have
holes in them,' and he'd say, 'Have you done this? Have
you done that?'" In light of the standard of living in Park
Ridge and similar bedroom communities of the fifties, it
is hard to imagine young Hillary being denied a pair of

shoes or, for that matter, walking around with holes in her shoes. Hillary was really in want of nothing. Hugh, a product of the Depression, had made sure of that.

For Hugh and his generation, the most convincing symbol of "making it" was owning a Cadillac, the true standard of excellence in American workmanship. General Motors itself was a symbol of American ingenuity and postwar industrial prosperity.

Halberstam illustrates how consumerism was reflected in the automobile.

> In the fifties bigger was better, and Americans, it seemed, wanted bigger cars every year. . . . General Motors had been waiting a long time for this market of abundance. They made car owners restless by playing off their broader aspirations. The Chevy was for blue-collar people. . . . The Pontiac was for more successful people. . . . The Olds was for the white-collar bureaucrat. . . . The Buick was for the town's doctor. . . . The Cadillac was for the top executive or owner of the local factory. Typically, when two brothers, Dick and Mac McDonald, after floundering most of their lives, finally succeeded in a big way with a small hamburger stand in San Bernadino, the first thing they did was buy a new Cadillac. That signaled that they had joined the proprietorial class.

Hugh Rodham was firmly and comfortably ensconced in this very same class. He had his Cadillac to prove it.

Hugh taught his children the value of hard work. He brought them back to the Scranton area and showed them the coal mines where his family and neighbors had toiled through the Depression. In fact, all three children were baptized in Scranton at the Court Street Methodist Church. The family would often spend vacations at Lake Winola in Scranton. Hugh wanted his children to know that not everyone was fortunate enough to live in a place like Park Ridge. The two boys often helped their father with the drapery business and other chores. Tony told the *Chicago Tribune* in 1993, "We were probably the only kids in the whole suburb that didn't get an allowance. We'd rake the leaves, cut the grass, pull weeds, shovel snow. All our friends would be going to a movie. After your errands, you'd walk in and say, 'Gee, Dad, I could use two or three dollars.' He'd flop another potato on your dinner plate and say, 'That's your reward.' "

"Big Hugh's presence really filled a room," Hillary's childhood friend, Betsy Johnson Ebeling, recalled for *Chicago* magazine in 1994. "He was a curmudgeon, exasperating and exhilarating all in the course of one evening. At dinner, he'd offer an opinion and wait for everybody to stomp on it. Hugh taught Hillary not to be afraid to speak her opinions."

Hillary, like her brothers, was given a variety of household chores. Dorothy Rodham stated that she was never paid for jobs around the house like some of her playmates. "As my husband always said, 'They eat and sleep for free! We're not going to pay them for it as well.' "

Due to Hugh's success in the drapery business, Dorothy did not have to work. She had not gone to college, and upon marrying Hugh in 1942, she dedicated herself to her family. Dorothy told *Paris Match*, "I spent all my time in the car then, I had three children, and each one had his or her little activity. I always encouraged them to do what they wanted to do. So I spent my time driving back and forth across town." Eventually, Dorothy did go back to school to earn a college degree. She took courses at junior colleges in the area when her children got older. At the urging of her son-in-law Bill Clinton, she studied philosophy.

In contrast to the sometimes gruff and demanding Hugh, Dorothy offered a support system for her children. Hillary explained, "It really was the classic parenting situation, where the mother is the encourager and the helper, and the father brings news from the outside world."

Hillary told *Family Circle* magazine that "she was spanked on occasion, or deprived of privileges." She added, "I was a quick learner. I didn't run afoul of my parents very often. They were strict about my respecting authority, and not just parental authority. My father's favorite saying was: 'You get in trouble at school, you get in trouble at home.'

"My parents really set high expectations for me and were rarely satisfied," Hillary explained.

> I always felt challenged. I always felt there was something else out there I could reach for. They expected us to do well and work as well as we knew how. And I felt very fortunate because as a girl growing up, I never felt anything but support from my family. Whatever I thought I could do and be, they supported. There was no distinction between me and my brothers or any barriers thrown up to me that I couldn't think about because I was a girl. If you work hard enough and you really apply yourself then you should be able to do whatever you choose to do.

"I never saw any difference in gender, as far as capabilities or aspirations were concerned," Dorothy Rodham told the *Washington Post*. "Just because Hillary was a girl didn't mean she should be limited. I don't know whether you could say that was unusual at the time. I guess it was more of an accepted role to stay within your scope."

"I was raised to be self-reliant and to be responsible but to know that I was part of a larger community to which I also have responsibilities," Hillary explained to *Parade* magazine. "I'm really grateful that both my parents, in different ways, gave me the support and structure that I needed to develop a sense of personal self-worth and security."

"We were raised with traditional midwestern values," Hillary's brother, Hugh, told *Good Housekeeping* magazine. "Family, church on Sunday, respect your elders, do

well in school, participate in sports." The three Rodham
kids were all active in a wide range of activities. Hillary
earned every merit badge available as a Brownie and Girl
Scout. She took ballet lessons at the age of ten and tried
to learn how to play the piano. She had limited success
with the piano and could usually be found playing all
sorts of sports and games, including tennis, softball, and
volleyball. The whole family went to the park one Sunday
afternoon to watch Hugh, Sr., teach young Hillary how to
hit a baseball. Hugh would not let his frustrated daughter off the hook, as the two spent hours at this until
Hillary was able to hit the ball. Hillary, as a child, was a
good athlete. According to her brother Tony, "She was a
terrific forward on the field hockey team until she went
to high school and got too studious."

Hillary's first ambition in life was to become an astronaut. She and her brothers would spend hours in the
basement in a makeshift spacecraft. Hillary was always in
the pilot's seat. "President Kennedy had just started the
drive to the moon and this was, like, in 1961, and I was
like, fourteen or so," Hillary told the *Washington Post*. "So
I wrote a letter to NASA and asked them what you would
do to be an astronaut. I told them something about
myself." When Hillary received word back from NASA
she was "infuriated" to learn that girls were not acceptable. The letter informed her that only boys could become astronauts. It was a shock to a young girl who had
been brought up by her parents to believe that she was
capable of achieving anything, regardless of the fact that
she was a girl. Hillary recalled, "I later realized that I
couldn't have become an astronaut anyway, because I
have such terrible eyesight. That somewhat placated me."

Young Hillary had other ambitions as well.

What really used to be the highlight of my week
was *Life* magazine on Fridays. It was filled with
these wonderful pictures—I remember a wonderful series on Margaret Bourke-White. They were so
big on pictures, any woman who was a photojour-

nalist or a foreign correspondent would get some
space in the magazine, because it would be kind of
sexy and unusual to have a woman doing this.
And, in the eighth grade, being a foreign correspondent was what I thought I wanted to be.

Hillary was a successful and exemplary student during her days in Park Ridge, routinely bringing home A's.
A classic grind, she had the reputation of a teacher's pet
throughout her elementary school years and in high
school. According to her brother Tony, "When she wasn't
studying, she was a lot of fun. But she was always studying."

Hugh and Dorothy had been drawn to Park Ridge
because of their interest in a quality school district for
their children. Hillary told Clinton biographer Charles
Allen, "I mean that's what the motivation was for the ex-
GIs after World War II, to try and find a good place to
raise your kids and send them to school. And I've often
kidded my father, who has never been a fan of taxes and
government, about moving to a place that had such high
property taxes to pay for school."

Dorothy, having not gone to college herself, wanted
the very best for her daughter and she felt that a college
education was essential for the empowerment of women
and, specifically, her daughter. "Learning for learning's
sake," Dorothy said. The realist Hugh was known to often declare, "Learning for earnings sake." Hugh had
escaped the drudgery of the Scranton mills courtesy of
the football scholarship he had earned to attend Penn
State. He was extremely tough on Hillary and her brothers and forced them to appreciate the value of a college
education. Hillary's brother Hugh would follow in his
father's footsteps, earning a football scholarship to Penn
State and playing as a back-up quarterback for the leg-
endary coach Joe Paterno.

"(My parents) told me that it was my obligation to go
to school, that I had an obligation to use my mind,"
Hillary told the *Arkansas Democrat*.

They told me that an education would enable me
to have a lot more opportunities in life, that if I
went to school and took it seriously and studied
hard, not only would I learn things and become
interested in the world around me, but I would
open up all kinds of doors to myself so that when
I was older I would have some control over my
environment. It was education for education's sake,
but also it was the idea that school was a real
pathway to a better opportunity.

Hillary attended the Eugene Field Grammar School,
which was three blocks from her home. When Hugh was
presented with Hillary's A-filled report cards through
these years, his usual response was, "You must go to a
pretty easy school." Elisabeth King was one of Hillary's
early influences. A strict, dour woman, Mrs. King taught
Hillary in both elementary school and junior high. In a
1992 *Washington Post* interview Ernest "Rick" Ricketts
stated that "Hillary was Mrs. King's favorite human being on Earth. When she moved on to Emerson Junior
High, she taught Hillary for two more years."

Hillary recalled in *Parade* magazine, "I had a sixth-
grade teacher, Elisabeth King, who went on with me to
junior high school as an English teacher. She was so
encouraging to us. She had us writing very long reports,
because she insisted that we had to learn how to express
ourselves. . . . If it hadn't been for my English teachers,
starting with Mrs. King and going all the way through
high school, I don't know that I'd be a very well-educated
person."

The Rodhams attended the First United Methodist
Church in Park Ridge. The church was located only a few
blocks away from Hillary's house. The church had recently built a new wing of classrooms to accommodate
the growing number of children in the congregation
brought on by the baby boom.

Hillary told Diane Huie Balay of the *Reporter*, a
Methodist publication,

Historically my father's family was always Methodist and took it very seriously. Mine is a family who
traces our roots back to Bristol, England, to the
coal mines and the Wesleys. So as a young child,
I would hear stories that my grandfather had heard
from his parents, who heard them from their parents who were all involved in the great evangelical
movement that swept England. When my personal
experience in church as a child was so positive—
not only the youth ministry work that I was part of
but a really active, vital, outreaching Sunday school
experience, lots of activities for children—there
was a sense in which the church was our second
home. We would walk up to the church, not only
to go to church but to play volleyball, to go to
potluck dinners, to be in plays. . . . It was just a
very big part of my life. And that kind of fellow-
ship was real important to me.

Interestingly, Hillary's parents had little involvement
with the church. Leon Osgood was Hillary's Sunday school
teacher during her senior year of high school. Osgood
has been a church leader for many years and a member
of the church all his life. When asked about Hugh
Rodham's involvement at First United, Osgood responded
that "he was not active in the church. I'm not sure he
even attended church. I was teaching there and have
been on the board of the church for many years. I remember Mrs. Rodham; she was not that active. Hugh
was not active at all. He traveled a lot on business, maybe
that was it."

Hillary Clinton has pointed to the Reverend Don
Jones as one of her earliest influences. Jones arrived as
the church's youth minister when Hillary was fourteen,
just entering high school. He had recently graduated
from divinity school at Drew University where he had
studied under the theologian Paul Tillich, whose theology was based on redefining the Christian's role in modern society. Thirty years old at the time, Jones brought

to the community something the young people of Park
Ridge called "The University of Life." Jones, with Tillich
as his mentor, felt the most significant role for his church
in society was to help the less fortunate. Hillary told
Newsweek, "He was just relentless in telling us that to be
a Christian did not just mean you were concerned about
your own personal salvation."

At the weekly Thursday night sessions, Jones attempted to open the eyes of the privileged youth of Park
Ridge. Introducing them to art and literature was part of
Jones's approach. He related theology and religion to art
and culture. He had discussions on Impressionism, and
exposed them to Picasso. The group was reading the
works of Tillich, Reinhold Niebuhr, Dietrich Bonhoffer,
and Soren Kierkegaard.

Jones told Judith Warner, the author of a 1993 Hillary
biography, "She was intellectual even then. She was open-
minded. She was curious, open to what life had to bring.
When I introduced her to a lot of new things, she was just
insatiable."

Jones had Hillary read J.D. Salinger's *The Catcher in
the Rye,* yet at the time, she was unable to comprehend
the meaning or understand the book. Jones remembers,
"She read the book, but she didn't say much about it, so
I didn't say much about it. But in college she had to read
it again for an English class and she wrote a letter to me
her sophomore year that said, 'I didn't tell you at the
time but when you had me read *Catcher in the Rye,* I
didn't like it, and moreover, I thought it was a little too
advanced for me. But now that I've read it a second time,
I realize, I think why you gave it to me."

The main character in *The Catcher in the Rye* is Holden
Caufield. A work of fiction, the book is an indictment of
the insincerity and phoniness of twentieth-century social
relations. Salinger readers today would certainly find
Hillary's college comments a bit ironic when they look at
the cosmetic and politically calculated transformations of
Hillary throughout her husband's political life. One can

only imagine how Salinger would describe a chance
meeting on the campaign trail between Holden Caufield
and a beaming, glad-handing Hillary.

Jones took the group into the city to see the under-
privileged of Chicago's South Side. Park Ridge was an
all-white community, and for many in the group, this was
their first interaction with blacks, Hispanics, and the street-
wise of Chicago's inner city. This type of experience served
as a way for Jones to expose the group to the less fortunate and to demonstrate to the group how fortunate they
were to be living in the comfort of the suburbs.

Hillary's friend and fellow group member, Sherry
Heiden, recalled to Judith Warner that "it was a time
when a lot of the idealism that was going to fuel the
sixties and early seventies was becoming known about.
We believed in the incredible social changes that can
happen if you change your perspective." One can only
imagine young Hillary and Sherry discussing their
"change of perspective" in the back seat of Hugh's Cadillac
on their way back from the ghetto to the suburbs.

But, Sherry Heiden does make the point that this
was, in fact, the time when America was beginning to
change its perspective on the inner-city poor. It was a
time when programs similar to Don Jones's "University
of Life" began telling young people that the affluence of
the fifties was bad, for it left a whole underclass of citizens victims of a Cadillac-guided society that cared nothing for the impoverished, which it had created. The poor
became victims; Hugh Rodham and the like became the
oppressors.

The group also had the opportunity to meet Martin
Luther King, Jr., after hearing him speak in 1962 at
Chicago's "Sunday Evening Club." Jones told the *Washington Post*, "Hillary still talks about it, remembers it viv-
idly. She says that afterward, I took everyone backstage
to meet Reverend King. Now I can't say that I recall this
precisely, but she says that I introduced King to each of
the kids, one by one."

Although a wide range of journalists have glorified
Jones's stay in Park Ridge, all have failed to mention that
his tenure in Park Ridge was not considered successful.
After only two years in Park Ridge, Jones was forced to
leave the community. Normally, a youth minister would
stay at least five to seven years in a given location. He
might have had an impact on Hillary, but the congregation as a whole were very disturbed with him. His popularity with the young people in town had little to do with
church teachings.

Bob Williams, a lifelong resident of Park Ridge and
former member of the church, remembers Jones's stint
in the town as "two extremely disruptive years." He recalls that the people of the town sarcastically referred to
Jones as the "Marvel from North Dakota." According to
Williams and others in Park Ridge, Jones made quite a
show of himself. "He looked like an All-American, blond
hair and tanned. He used to drive around town in a
convertible—the girls salivated." Williams stated that he
was "amazed" when he learned that First Lady Hillary
considered Jones one of her mentors. "I understand that
Don went on and did some other things, but from what
I knew of him then, if you were picking mentors—he's
one you would not pick. People were leaving the church
because of his teachings."

Leon Osgood knew Jones well.

> I liked Don and considered him a good friend. I
> felt sorry for him then; I thought he was at least
> well meaning. But he got under the skin of the
> older members of the church and they forced him
> to leave. He was young and show-offy, driving
> around in his convertible. We had a large youth
> group and the feeling was that he was having an
> influence on quite a few people. The older mem-
> bers were quite concerned, and asked him to leave.

Osgood wrote a recommendation for Jones after the
young minister's unfortunate demise in Park Ridge. He

felt it was "the least I could do for the guy." He recalls that it was for a post in New Jersey. "I liked Don. I actually agreed with him on some of his teachings. But, I was one of the few. His new ideas on sexuality and things like that were not welcome at the church. I was glad to see him get that other job. I felt sorry for him."

Paul Carlson remembers returning to Park Ridge after graduate school. He went to the Methodist church to hear Jones speak and was shocked at what he heard. "I approached him after the service and suggested we get together. I was teaching at Maine East at the time and was concerned. I had lunch with him the next day and explained that I wasn't at all amused with his message, that it was not a Christian speech. He really gave no defense of what he had said. He was as left-wing as they come." Carlson recalls that he used to "spar quite often with Jones."

In July of 1994, Osgood met up with Jones again. "Don was here in Park Ridge recently with a film crew from France doing something on Hillary. I went by to see him, he gave me a picture of him and his wife with Bill and Hillary. He seems to be doing well for himself now."

Hillary graduated from Maine South High School in Park Ridge in 1965. She had spent three years at Maine East High School prior to her senior year. Maine South had been built to deal with the growing number of students as a result of the baby boom. Hillary's class was the first to graduate from the new school. Maine East had been built in 1930 and was a testament to the high priority that education was given in the community. The school was modeled after UCLA's Westwood campus. It is a large school, complete with an impressive gymnasium and swimming pool, facilities most small colleges would envy. Even back in the fifties, the school had its own radio station. The nineties have even brought the school its own television station. The newly built Maine South was, and still is, equally impressive.

Interestingly, there is no special mention or display of First Lady Hillary anywhere at Maine East. At Maine South there are photographs taken during a 1992 campaign visit. The name Hillary Rodham can be found on a plaque located in the foyer, as well. She is listed as one of twelve students from the Class of '65 that were awarded a Goodwill Award. The award is given annually to students who did the most to promote Maine South.

Hillary had fine teachers growing up, such as Paul Carlson. He has been teaching history and government at Maine East since the 1950s. With a master's degree from William and Mary, he is an example of the quality faculty that was drawn to Park Ridge. Carlson is the resident historian and raconteur for Maine East. His classroom is a standing testimony to his years of dedication to teaching. Complete with bleacher seats from Wrigley Field and historical memorabilia, the room is more a museum than a classroom. Prominent portraits of the presidents, as well as such people as Douglas McArthur and Winston Churchill, grace the walls. There are also two permanently empty seats in Carlson's class: one for the many young men that have died in America's wars, and another for one of his students who was killed tragically in an automobile accident. The empty seats in the front of the class serve as a daily reminder of the fragility of life.

In room 338, just down the hall from Carlson's present classroom, Hillary had been a student of his some thirty years ago. He remembers Hillary very well, and even knows exactly where she sat. "That was Hillary's freshman year, seventh hour, she sat in the first row, fifth seat." Carlson remembers Hillary as a vibrant young girl and an excellent student.

Carlson is a conservative Republican who has little use for Hillary's politics. Yet, he says, "that's no reason to bash her. She was a wonderful student here at Maine East. She wrote a 75-page paper for me, complete with 150 note cards, and 50 sources on the bibliography. It was extremely well-done; I can't get kids today to do something like that. This was freshman year; she was probably only fourteen years old at the time." Carlson's praise for the Hillary he knew extends beyond scholastic abilities. "She was always well-groomed, respectful, and polite. Hillary always spoke forcefully—polite but aggressive. She was not the type that ever crabbed about being overworked. She was very capable, very intelligent, and very open. She was a very fine young lady."

Carlson wrote a lengthy letter to First Lady Hillary in the fall of 1993. "I told her it was refreshing to see her speak out. I urged her to keep talking, keep up the dialogue. I don't agree with what she has to say; she knows that. But it's important for our leaders to speak out. I told her to keep up the dialogue. Keep up the controversy." He received a warm response from Hillary five months later. She apologized for the delay in responding and explained that his letter had been lost in the volumes of White House mail. She invited him to the White House and gave a phone number that she said was more private than the switchboard. "She urged me to call the next time I was in Washington."

Hillary's other teachers in high school echoed the thoughts of Carlson. Kenneth Reese told Judith Warner,

> She was a forceful person, confident, obviously motivated, and she was able to get things done. She was active and she was a leader. The kids just kind of automatically looked up to her because she spoke out for things that she believed in. She would take an unpopular stance on something and would be willing to be in the minority position, and be able to support that position. . . . It was just that she was confident in her own skills—she was bright and had strong convictions and was able to follow through on them.

Rick Ricketts recalled Hillary's interaction with Maine South's principal, Dr. Clyde Watson, for *Chicago* magazine in 1994:

> Hillary wanted the student council election in the spring of 1965 to be a carbon copy of the national conventions—nominating speeches, demonstrations, signs. She had all this material written down, and a group of us went to see Dr. Watson. The administration was very conservative, and they were taking away the extracurricular things we'd had at Maine East, like all-school assemblies. But Dr. Watson was completely blown away by Hillary's plan, and he approved everything. She recruited everybody to work on it, and it turned out to be exactly how she'd envisioned it.

Hillary was involved in a variety of activities. Her senior picture in the yearbook is accompanied by a long list of activities, ranging from student government to something called the Cultural Values Committee. She can also be found in her junior year as a member of the Sportsmanship Committee, chaired by her close friend Rick Ricketts. The only person mentioned more in the book is Tim Sheldon, quarterback of the football team and senior class president. Sheldon is now a judge living in Geneva, Illinois.

Hillary's yearbook photo is of a confident and attractive young woman. In only one picture of her four high-school yearbooks is Hillary seen wearing glasses. Her self-consciousness and attention to her appearance during high school stand in marked contrast to what she would become. In college Hillary would gain weight, begin to wear glasses, and adopt the dressing habits of the times, but teachers and classmates never fail to mention that Hillary was always well dressed and well groomed during high school.

Penny Pullen is a former Republican state legislator who represented Park Ridge for many years, and is a long-time pro-life leader in Illinois. Her conservative views are representative of those of the Park Ridge community. She and Hillary knew each other in high school; both were members of the National Honor Society. Pullen

remembers Hillary as being very political, even back in
high school.

> Everyone knew Hillary. She was on all the commit-
> tees, and always involved in all sorts of activities.
> There was a real mix in high school of what we
> called the "greasers" and "skinheads." The skinheads
> were the class leaders. Hillary and her friends made
> up this group. The greasers were the troublemak-
> ers. She was very social, very conscious of her ap-
> pearance and of her status. She was a leader; she
> certainly stood out as someone with potential.

> I do remember Hillary talking to one of her friends
> about a good citizenship award that was given out
> by the Daughters of the American Revolution.

> It struck me as odd, even at the time, that Hillary
> was more or less plotting a strategy to get certain
> recommendations from certain teachers. She
> seemed to be lobbying for the award. This was an
> award that was conferred on someone, not some-
> thing that was competed for. Because she knew it
> would look good, for college or whatever, she was
> actively pursuing the award. She was determined
> to get it.

Hillary was, in fact, awarded the prize.

According to another female classmate quoted in
Chicago magazine, "Hillary was so take-charge, so determined, so involved in every single activity, that you'd
think, 'Why don't you chill out a bit? Why don't you give
somebody else a chance?' I always felt that Hillary thought
she knew what was best, so that's what everybody else
should do. It's the same attitude with health care—Hillary
knows what's best for the country, and we should just go
along."

Penny Pullen also confirms that Hillary was in fact a
"Goldwater Girl." "Goldwater made sense to us in Park
Ridge. Hillary was a skinhead, too. That was all part of
it. She was after status and recognition. Our town in the

sixties was staunchly Republican. Not backing Goldwater would have been an unpopular stance for someone striving to be so popular."

Indeed, Hillary was a strong supporter of her father's Republican party. She wore the "Goldwater Girl" sash at rallies and helped organize students for Republican events. Another classmate, Betsy Johnson Ebeling, said that she and Hillary both read Goldwater's *The Conscience of a Conservative*. "Hillary and I both read the book and found it very striking—Goldwater's championing of the individual."

Hillary Rodham was voted by her classmates as Most Likely to Succeed upon graduation from Maine South. She was a mature, responsible, and active young woman. Her parents and teachers had done their job well. Yet, later in life, the media singled out Don Jones as her mentor, and Hillary did nothing to blunt that impression. To recognize any of the dedicated outstanding teachers at Maine East and South High Schools would be to undermine a myth.

In a 1993 post-election edition of *People*, Don Jones was highlighted as one of the "seminal influences in her life." This article, like many others, goes to great lengths to chronicle the long and lasting friendship of Hillary and Jones. But, in a photograph of Jones in an easy chair poring over a personal letter from his protégé, a piece of evidence about their real relationship is inadvertently provided. With the use of a magnifying glass, words can be seen on the back of the page held by Jones. Although the words can only be read with great difficulty, they can be made out: "If you are not my old friend then greetings and keep up the good work." Right underneath is the signature "Hillary Rodham."

This is not the message one would send to someone who supposedly had so much influence, even one that has been out of touch for several years. At the very least, Jones's influence on Hillary has been greatly exaggerated. The exaggeration has not been discouraged by either of

them, presumably because it serves the interests of both.
All the available evidence suggests, however, that Jones
was the source of no great awakening or enlightenment.
Hillary was an ambitious conformist, totally accepting of
her environment and the values of her community. Her
assertiveness was not a challenge to authority, but instead was encouraged at the dinner table and in class.

Liberals have needed Don Jones to provide a point
at which Hillary departed from the repression and closed-
mindedness of middle-class suburbia. Likewise, conservatives have needed Jones as the political Svengali who
transformed the Goldwater girl into a left-wing radical.
Neither viewpoint is correct.

Jones could not cause a transformation in Hillary
because as subsequent chapters of her life show, she never
has been transformed. The only thing that has changed
in Hillary's life is the world around her. She has been
remarkably consistent in her reactions to people and
events, starting at Eugene Field Grammar School. Always, she has pursued status within her peer group, drop-
ping previously articulated beliefs with only a hint of self-
consciousness.

That accounts for a significant part of the negative
"Talk of the Town" reaction in 1993. It wasn't so much
that Hillary had rejected many of the values cherished in
Park Ridge in her role as feminist. Any American town
would be proud to produce a First Lady, feminist or not.
Rather, it was a more generalized sentiment that Hillary
wasn't really what she and her adorers in the national
media portrayed her to be. After all, you can't fool the
people you grew up with.

Hillary has variously praised and demeaned her
hometown, depending on the circumstances and audience, a fact that has not gone unnoticed in Park Ridge.
A leftist First Lady might have her portrait hanging in
the library but not an opportunist. For many in Park
Ridge, the fake southern accent on "60 Minutes" was all
they needed to hear.

*Hillary's commencement speech would get her national attention—
and her picture in* Life *magazine.*

(Photo by Lee Balterman/Life Magazine © Time Warner Inc.)

Two

Wellesley College

Maine South teacher Paul Carlson can remember the first time he saw Hillary after she left high school. In the summer of 1969, just after she graduated from Wellesley College, Hillary appeared on the "Irv Kupcinet Show," a political program on the Chicago Public Broadcasting station. Carlson turned to his mother and said, "Hillary's become a radical." Carlson recalls, "She was wearing wire glasses, granny clothes, and had her hair pulled back. This was definitely not the same person I had taught."

High-school classmate Penny Pullen remembers seeing the same show. "I remember saying, 'Wow, look at Hillary.' She was a raving liberal."

Hillary entered college in the fall of 1965, before the emergence of the youth and anti-war movements. The civil rights movement was in full swing and liberalism was on the ascent, but the full-blown counterculture would not arrive until her junior and senior years.

Wellesley College, located on a beautiful campus just outside of Boston, is one of the "Seven Sisters." Small, private, and expensive, these northeastern women's colleges have traditionally educated the daughters of the nation's rich and powerful. Unlike Vassar, for example, Wellesley resisted the social changes of the sixties and seventies, and did not go co-ed.

Hillary did not visit Wellesley prior to her arrival in the fall of 1965. While most of her high-school classmates stayed in Chicago and the Midwest for college,

Hillary decided to go East. In her senior year, there were two young graduate students from Chicago's Northwestern University serving as student teachers at Maine South. One had gone to Smith; the other went to Wellesley. Hillary was so impressed with these young women that she applied to both Smith and Wellesley. She was accepted to both and chose Wellesley.

Janet Altman Spragens, a Wellesley graduate, remembered to *Washington Post* reporter Donnie Radcliffe, the author of *Hillary Rodham Clinton: A First Lady for Our Time*, "I just said Wellesley offered an extraordinarily high-quality education, that it had enormous resources, stressed the importance of women's education and women's role in society, that very talented women went there, and that I was sure she would make important lifetime friends."

Like other elite colleges, the political atmosphere at Wellesley can accurately be described as liberal, both in 1965 and now. But, it would be a mistake to put Wellesley at the forefront of the social and sexual revolution of the sixties. Indeed, the women of Wellesley were fighting a successful rear-guard action to preserve single-sex education, while most of the other Eastern elitist schools were adopting co-education.

Wellesley's identification as a women's college is deeply seated and zealously guarded by students, faculty, and alumni alike. In 1969, student Judith Maguire described her feelings in the *Wellesley News*, the student newspaper. "I like the lack of competition here. . . . With the introduction of men, who are naturally competitive and must be to find a job, this atmosphere would be lost. . . . I can only see that the quality of the education for Wellesley women would fall if men were added to this society." Another student, Chris Larsen, described it this way: "Wellesley College offers women the opportunity to educate themselves in an atmosphere free of androcentric distractions."

During Hillary's senior year, the school experimented with something called Co-Ed Week. According to some accounts, the experiment was less than a success. Samuel Seskin (Yale '72) made the trip from New Haven for the much-ballyhooed event. He wrote back to the Wellesley campus of his experiences.

> The accommodations and curfews are two examples of uncompromising students and administration. Although the latter's rudeness is more blatant, the former's is more serious for its subtlety. I came here only asking to share in a coeducational living experience, but found the opportunities for inter-action pitifully few. . . . My stay has been brief, but unfortunately too long. Perhaps it would have been better if I had not come at all.

In a letter entitled "Successful Alienation," another Yale man named Philip Rich wrote,

> Throughout the half of Co-Ed week which I at-tended, a spirit of artificiality pervaded the cam-pus. Forced situations were contrived and even at these the number of co-eds usually exceeded the number of girls. The lack of women in the midst of 1700 women was explained away as shyness, but your extreme reticence seemed little more than rudeness. Your main success in holding Co-Ed Week was alienating these men who had taken the time to cut classes and come to Wellesley. The barren-ness of the whole situation was summed up when a guy from (Boston College) came up to me at Pomeroy Friday night and said, "My friends and I have had it with these snobs. We're going drinking. . . . Wanna come?"

Surprisingly, the issue of men on campus was still alive twenty years later. In 1992, two students wrote a letter to the *News* describing the experience of a male friend who was unable to find a friend's car.

Thinking he was upset when he returned to the
dorm because he was unable to find the car, we
soon discovered that it was the feeling of objecti-
fication that had overwhelmed him in his search.
He was glared at and the subject of many scowls as
he was unable to walk into any building on campus. Bob felt as if he was the criminal element of
Wellesley College. We naively thought that by having a suite with our own shower, we could shield
our male friends from the harsh reality of
Wellesley's "non-user-friendly" treatment of men.

The letter concludes, "Yes Wellesley is a women's
college, but we still cannot deny that men are a large
part of the world's population. . . . The next time you see
a man on campus, remember that he could be your
brother or your friend and treat him with the consideration he deserves."

During the sixties, the women of Wellesley were not
only successfully isolated from men, but also from racial
minorities. Hillary's class of four hundred had just six
African-Americans. The Vietnam War, which was often
criticized as a "poor boys' war," had less impact there
than on other campuses. There were very few poor at
Wellesley, and even fewer boys. The protests and student
strikes of Berkeley or Columbia were unthinkable.

Even if the Wellesley women did not get swept up in
radical politics, dramatic events like the assassinations of
Martin Luther King, Jr., and Bobby Kennedy could not
be ignored. The youth culture was coming into full bloom,
and included politics, music, social mores, and dress.
Activism was part of the fashion of the times, and Wellesley
students were never indifferent to fashion. The women
of Wellesley felt they had to get involved somehow, create some type of dissent.

Hillary's undergraduate years were characterized by
her conscientious studying, her emergence as a student
leader (including her election to student body president),
and her involvement in partisan politics. The reactions

of Paul Carlson and Penny Pullen to the 1969 Irv Kupcinet appearance suggest Hillary underwent an ideological transformation at Wellesley, an assertion made repeatedly by journalists, both sympathetic and critical.

There is, however, little evidence for it. Her college interests—the studying as well as the on and off campus politics—were the same as her high-school interests. Hillary continued to work hard at what brought her status within her peer group, and among those who could help her at a later time. The change came in her environment, from a conservative midwestern suburb to a liberal New England women's college.

According to "Eldie" Acheson, the granddaughter of Secretary of State Dean Acheson, and one of Hillary's long-time friends from Wellesley, Hillary's liberalism took root soon after she arrived on campus. She credits this "right-thinking" to "a ton of younger assistant professors and lecturers and instructors who came to that college with a lot of new ideas and some very aggressive, advocacy oriented ways of teaching." According to Hillary biographer Norman King, Acheson stated, "What happens to everybody at Wellesley? They become right-thinking."

For many of Wellesley's daughters of affluence, their professed liberalism is not exactly pure. A month before Acheson was nominated for a Justice Department post in 1993, she resigned her membership at The Country Club in Brookline, Massachusetts. It has no black members, and at the time she became a member, women were not granted full membership. She kept her membership, however, in the Longwood Cricket Club, which has no blacks out of 850 members, and the Badminton and Tennis Club in Boston, which has no blacks out of 410 members.

As a campus leader, Hillary fought for such "radical" causes as a better system for returning library books and for changes in the academic course requirement system. Hillary told a group of alumnae in April 1968, "The cry for responsibility in shaping one's education and one's life has real consequences for Wellesley, academically and non-academically." She went on to proudly cite the role that student government had played in the pass-fail option and changes in the sign-out and parietal regulations. Hillary cited these as "significant steps initiated by student action."

Hillary also became involved with weightier issues, including the war. "Hillary would usually run those meetings," recalled her political science professor, Alan Schecter. "I remember that a lot of them were held in the chapel. It was never a case of people pounding their fists on tables. There was never a suggestion that we should all march downtown. Hillary and most of the other students were against the war, but everything was approached in a very pragmatic way. I'm sure people on neighboring campuses blanched at our lack of radicalism at Wellesley."

Ruth Adams, president of Wellesley, told *The Boston Globe,* "She was liberal in her attitudes, but she definitely was not a radical. She was, as a number of her generation were, interested in effecting change, but from within rather than outside the system. They were not a group that wanted to go out and riot and burn things. They wanted to go to law school, get good degrees and change from within."

Hillary met Geoffrey Shields, a Harvard freshman, in the fall of her first year at Wellesley. He was from Lake Forest, Illinois, a wealthy suburb of Chicago. The two would date off and on for the next three years. He, like Hillary, was a Midwest conservative upon his arrival in Boston. Shields did not view Hillary as either conservative or liberal at this point, and by no means a radical. He told David Maraniss, the author of a sympathetic Bill Clinton biography, that he felt Hillary was "largely non-ideological" and that her mind was a "clean slate." According to Shields she seemed "very interested in exploring political ideas, interested in the process as op-

posed to the ideology of politics." Shields remembers
that "recognition was important to her."

During her four years at Wellesley, Hillary's partisanship seemed as flexible as her ideology. She was elected
president of the campus Young Republicans in her freshman year. As a sophomore, she still identified herself as
a Republican, but expressed admiration for the liberal
GOP mayor of New York City, John Lindsay. In October
1966, the student newspaper reported that Hillary
Rodham, president of the Young Republicans, was re-
cruiting volunteers for the races of two liberal Republicans. Massachusetts Attorney General Edward Brooke was
running for the Senate, and Margaret Heckler from the
town of Wellesley was a candidate for Congress. Hillary
implored her classmates that there were "opportunities
for all types of people. . . . The girl who doesn't want to
go out and shake hands can type letters and do general
office work."

Hillary spent the summer following her sophomore
year as a researcher/babysitter for a Wellesley professor
who was writing a book on the Vietnam War. According
to Shields, who would visit Hillary at the professor's beach
house on Lake Michigan that summer, Hillary had become a strong opponent of the war and was no longer a
Republican.

Upon her return to Wellesley in the fall of 1967, she
campaigned for the liberal anti-war candidate Eugene
McCarthy in neighboring New Hampshire in the Democratic primary against Hubert Humphrey. When
Humphrey secured the nomination, she campaigned for
him in Massachusetts and New Hampshire in his bid
against Richard Nixon.

Judith Warner asserts that this ostensive switch to the
Democratic party caused Hugh Rodham distress.

> Outside the sheltered enclave of the progres-
> sive women's college, life wasn't always so trium-
> phant. Hillary's conversion to McCarthy's ideals
> put her in direct conflict with her conservative

father. When fights flared between them, the bottom line always was politics. Hillary's switch to the Democratic party was not, one might say, in a time of university takeovers, "tuning out" or "turning on," a major rebellion. But in her family it was, and the dissenting words at the dinner table sometimes cut deep.

It must have come as some relief for Hugh when Hillary was chosen, along with thirteen other students, for the Wellesley Internship Program, a project that sent Wellesley students to Capitol Hill for the summer. After campaigning for McCarthy and Humphrey, Hillary was now spending the summer of 1968 working for the House Republican Conference in Washington. The group of interns worked on a variety of research projects. Hillary was paid through the office of Harold Collier, the Republican congressman who represented Park Ridge. She traveled to Miami that summer for the Republican National Convention as a supporter of the governor of New York, Nelson Rockefeller.

She also witnessed the unrest at the Democratic National Convention that summer in Chicago. She was home in Park Ridge at the time, and she and high-school friend Betsy Johnson took the train into the city to take in the events. Johnson remembers seeing "kids our age getting their heads beaten in. And the police were doing the beating."

Hillary returned for her senior year as the president of College Government, having been elected the previous spring in a campuswide election, overcoming two opponents. Her campaign statement in the *News* stressed process: "A student government that does not deal with academic issues is an anachronism. I have been working through the Constitution Revision Committee on a plan for a joint student-faculty board to consider ideas of curricular innovation and to evaluate individual proposals for independent studies."

Hillary worked long and hard to achieve the presidency. As a sophomore, she represented her class in College Government, and as a junior she had been a prestigious Vil Junior, who act as counselors to freshman. Hillary not only represented her dorm as a Vil Junior, but was chairman of all Vil Juniors. Roommate Johanna Bronson recalled to *The Boston Globe* that "Hillary was quite careful about what to do next (in her senior year). She knew she wanted to be involved in student government and Vil Juniors would connect her to younger students."

Not all were enamored with her leadership. The editor of the *News*, Penny Ortner McPhee, remembered, "There were probably some students among us who felt she had too good a rapport with the Administration. She was maybe more willing to compromise, to compromise too soon."

In February of 1969, the *News* criticized her priorities. "We are tired of high school campaigns for more spirit, awareness, and participation"—a reference to an announcement in a previous issue about an essay contest. Contestants were to answer the question "What is School Spirit?" and to send any suggestions on "how to perk up school spirit" to President Hillary Rodham.

A couple of months later, the paper questioned her means. An editorial entitled "Backroom Politics" accused her of bypassing the normal procedure of elections to select her friends for student government posts. "The habit of appointing friends and members of the 'in'-group should be halted immediately in order that knowing people in power does not become a prerequisite to officeholding." It went on to accuse her of "elitism" and concluded that "ends do not justify means."

Like Maine South High School, Wellesley had its own caste system. In high school, Hillary and her fellow skinheads looked down on the greasers. At Wellesley, Hillary was a "cool," who considered herself a cut above

the "jerks" and "ughs." One classmate told Donnie
Radcliffe, "If you were somebody from Scarsdale High
School, I'm sure you found it easier to be around her
than if you were from someplace like Enid, Oklahoma. It
could be very intimidating."

Through all the politicking, Hillary remained an
excellent student and, as in high school, was a teacher's
pet. A classmate said, "She cultivated relationships with
teachers and administrators even more than with students."

She wrote her senior thesis on community action
programs that aimed to help the poor. Her thesis advisor, Alan Schecter, felt that she began the project with
the conservative view that the poor should be responsible
for taking control of their own lives. But, after a year of
work on the thesis, her views became more in tune with
her professors and the times. According to Schecter, her
final thesis was that poor people could organize themselves and sometimes achieve progress in the short term,
but that dramatic changes in the structure of society were
necessary to ameliorate poverty.

Hillary's ambition had always been to become a lawyer. She would ultimately become a high-priced corporate lawyer earning over two hundred thousand dollars
annually for the Rose Law Firm in Little Rock. Yet, at
this point in her life, she talked about "helping the poor"
and "improving the system." She had the grades and
credentials to have her pick of the elitist East Coast law
schools and would ultimately choose Yale. Her adviser,
Alan Schecter, himself a graduate of Yale Law School,
remembers that he steered Hillary there because the
school put less emphasis on how to make a lot of money
as a lawyer and more on the worth of social activism.

In a bow to the times, Wellesley broke tradition and
planned to have not one, but two commencement speakers, one a distinguished American and the other a student. As president of the College Government, Hillary
was selected to give the address. The administration asked

that her remarks be appropriate for the occasion and express the views of her classmates.

The other commencement speech was given by Massachusetts Sen. Edward Brooke, for whom Hillary had campaigned as a sophomore. Brooke was the first black United States senator since Reconstruction. He was a liberal Republican and an annoyance to Nixon and many others in the Republican party.

Senator Brooke, in his remarks, addressed the tumult of the age: "Dissent and protest are essential ingredients in the democratic concoction. Without them an open society becomes a contradiction in terms, and representative government becomes as stagnant as despotism. Yet there is a narrow line between productive dissent and counter-productive disruption."

Brooke addressed social ills.

> If one takes what might be called the summary problem of our society, the persistence of poverty amid affluence, there has been measurable progress in these years. In 1959 some 22 percent of the nation's households were poor; by 1967 those below the poverty line totaled 13.3 percent. One can properly state, in viewing this trend, that the bottle of poverty is still more than half full, but it is worth noting that it is less full than before.

> Racial and social injustice is being seen in concrete terms, as a root cause of human misery and as a principle obstacle to the further development of this nation. Poverty, hunger, unemployment, inferior education, inadequate health care—these grave inequities are now being recognized for what they are, the responsibility of society as a whole as well as the individuals involved.

At the conclusion of Brooke's remarks, the president of Wellesley College, Ruth Adams, introduced Hillary in glowing terms. "In four years she has combined academic ability with active service to the College, her junior year having served as a Vil Junior, and then as a member of Senate and during the past year as President of College Government and presiding officer of the Senate. She is also cheerful, good-humored, good company, and a good friend to all of us, and it is a great pleasure to present to this audience Miss Hillary Rodham."

What followed was quite unexpected. The tenor of Hillary's remarks was anything but good-natured. Aside from the fact that her speech was at times barely coherent, she digressed from her prepared remarks to chide Brooke as if he were some sort of reactionary.

"What does it mean to hear that 13.3% of the people in this country are below the poverty line? That's a percentage. We're not interested in social reconstruction; it's human reconstruction. How can we talk about percentages and trends? The complexities are not lost in our analysis, but perhaps they're just put into what we consider a more human and eventually a more progressive perspective."

She challenged Brooke's distinction between productive dissent and counterproductive disruption. "Every protest, every dissent, whether it's on an individual paper or a Founder's parking lot demonstration, is unabashedly an attempt to forge an identity in this particular age. The attempt at forging for many of us over the past four years has meant coming to terms with our humanness."

Brooke must have found the experience a little bizarre. An advocate of liberalism and civil rights, Brooke had also actually overcome racism to get elected to the Senate by an overwhelmingly white constituency. Additionally, he was an outspoken opponent of his own president on the Vietnam War. This did not stop him from being assailed as insufficiently "progressive" by the gowned twenty-one-year-old white suburbanite.

For good measure, Hillary offended most of the parents present, particularly the fathers who had paid for their daughters' educations. "There are some things we feel, feelings that our prevailing, acquisitive and competitive corporate life, including tragically our universities, is not the way of life for us. We're searching for more immediate, ecstatic, and penetrating modes of living." One can only imagine the dismay of the successful Hugh Rodham listening to his daughter's confused, anti-corporate, anti-success rhetoric.

While her attack on Brooke may have been considered courageous by some, it would have been more effective if it had made sense. For instance, "Within the context of a society that we perceive—now we can talk about reality, and I would like to talk about reality sometime, authentic reality, inauthentic reality, and what we have to accept of what we see—but our perception of it is that it hovers between the possibility of disaster and the potentiality for imaginatively responding to men's needs."

Long sentences, sprinkled with the catch-phrases of the times, seemed to lead nowhere. It was as if the words themselves were more important than the information they conveyed. It was ideological fashion. At the podium was Hillary Rodham, a "radical" wannabe.

The commencement speech might be considered by some conclusive proof of a transformation. But, even if it was not manifested at Wellesley, the times had become more extreme. Experimentation in sex, drugs, music, and politics was reaching its peak. What was radical in 1966 was considered tame in 1969. With the help of Charlie Manson, the innocence of the Summer of Love in 1967 was already a memory. King and Kennedy were dead. The peace movement had failed to elect an anti-war president in 1968. In short, by 1969 the counterculture was in a state of confusion. And, in a revolution that is going badly, there is only one option—to get even more extreme. The rhetoric of 1969 was produced under these circumstances, and that is why it seems so strange today.

Hillary was getting ready for a new stage, and she knew it was to be far different from the one at Wellesley.

She was headed for Yale Law School, a truly radical place, where even the administrators and faculty were on the cutting edge of the political and social movements of the day. The Wellesley commencement was a place to make her mark and she succeeded. Her photo appeared in *Life* magazine along with a short excerpt from her speech. The controversy over her remarks was enough to be noticed beyond Wellesley, but it was not, of course, akin to occupying a building or some other act that might preclude her from graduating.

As real radicals were going underground, Hillary spent her summer vacation backpacking in Alaska. At this point, it appears that Hillary had little or no financial worries. As chastened as Hugh Rodham might have been by the commencement speech, he still made it financially possible for Hillary to do as she pleased.

Geoffrey Shields told David Maraniss that he heard from Hillary shortly after her graduation. "She said it had been hard for her to come around and make what was both a political statement and a personal attack. There was some exhilaration but also nervous questioning about whether it had really been the right thing to do. She realized what she had done was important. But when it was over she wondered about what she had said. She asked, 'Did I go too far?' "

Three

Yale Law School

Suspected of being a police informant, Black Panther Alex Rackley was tied to a bed in a New Haven apartment, burned with hot water, and then driven to the woods outside the city, where he was shot and left dead in a swamp. It was May of 1969, the same time as the Wellesley commencement, and Rackley's murder made national headlines. Within a few days, eight Black Panthers were arrested and charged with kidnapping and murder, including George Sams, who implicated Panther National Chairman Bobby Seale.

Members of the Black Panther Party for Self Defense, or the Black Panthers for short, advocated violence in the cause of black self-determination. Often photographed with weapons, the Panthers made good on their reputation. By 1969, they had been involved in a string of violent incidents around the country. Panther theoretician Eldridge Cleaver outlined the group's ideology in his book, *Soul on Ice*. Among other things, Cleaver justified the rape of white women by black men as a political act of protest against white oppression.

Two of the arrested Panthers, George Sams and Warren Kimbro, cooperated with prosecutors in exchange for a reduction in their charges from first to second degree murder. The two testified that along with a third Panther, named Lonnie McLucas, they took Rackley out to a country road and killed him. McLucas corroborated Kimbro's own testimony that Kimbro shot Rackley then gave the gun to McLucas and told him to shoot Rackley again to make sure that he was dead. McLucas never denied shooting Rackley.

The ironclad case against the Panthers did not preclude demonstrations of support on their behalf by a large number of white Yale undergraduate and law students and faculty. Even Kingman Brewster, the president of Yale, maintained, "I am skeptical of the ability of black revolutionaries to achieve a fair trial anywhere in the United States."

When Hillary arrived at Yale in the fall of 1969, New Haven was caught up in the upcoming trial of the Black Panthers. The New Haven courthouse, situated on the edge of the Yale campus, would become the scene of many demonstrations and disturbances. The National Guard was called in as store windows were being boarded up by the local merchants. The Yale Law School quadrangle was transformed into a sort of left-wing flea market, with tents devoted to various causes. Many students did not attend classes, but instead took part in teach-ins and listened to speakers representing the Students for a Democratic Society (SDS) and other radical groups. The Black Panthers and their white supporters on campus were certainly "radicals" in the context of American politics, and they certainly appeared that way to the rest of the country. But, in reality, there were no "radicals" at Yale. Most everyone, including students, faculty, and administrators, espoused radical politics. The Panthers and SDS were considered mainstream. As at other key points in her life, Hillary had no trouble adapting to her new surroundings.

In the spring of 1970, a new law journal was published called the *Yale Review of Law and Social Action*, and it devoted significant attention to the McLucas murder trial. The Board of Editors consisted of nine students, including Hillary Rodham. An article by James F. Blumstein and James Phelan proposed "political migration to a single state for the purpose of gaining political control and establishing a living laboratory for experiment." The authors asserted, "Experimentation with drugs, sex, individual lifestyles or radical rhetoric and action within the society is an insufficient alternative. Total experimentation is necessary. New ideas and values must be taken out of heads and transformed into reality."

During the summer of 1970, Lonnie McLucas was found guilty of conspiracy to murder Alex Rackley and was sentenced to twelve to fifteen years in prison. Six other Panthers pled guilty to lesser charges. The charges against Bobby Seale were eventually dismissed. Lawyers for McLucas attempted to portray their client as an unwitting accomplice who was simply following the orders of Sams out of fear for his own life. They argued in vain that McLucas did not know why they were driving an already burned and tortured Rackley out to the woods.

The entire fall 1970 issue of the *Review*, which by this time listed Hillary Rodham as associate editor, was dedicated to the Black Panther trial. An illustration portrays police as long-nosed pigs. The word *fascist* was emblazoned on the uniform of one of the gun-toting creatures, and their thoughts were revealed in a cartoonist's balloon which read, "Niggers, niggers, niggers." Another illustration was of a squealing pig being slaughtered by gunfire under the caption "SEIZE THE TIME!" The journal posed the question "What is a Pig?" and answered, "A low natured beast that has no regard for law, justice or the rights of people; a creature that bites the hand that feeds it; a foul depraved traducer, usually found masquerading as the victim of an unprovoked attack."

The *Review* provided McLucas a forum:

> A few other revolutionaries have been tried by the courts of this system without any real hope of obtaining justice or achieving retribution. I consider myself to be a true revolutionary in every sense of the word. I feel that these circumstances are a replay of past circumstances that revolutionaries have been

involved in, due to the fact that the system hasn't changed noticeably over the past 350 years. . . . The laws that I was tried by were made a long time ago, and because of that fact alone, I wasn't given a fair trial. It would have been better if the laws had been revolutionized laws.

Later in her life, Hillary's supporters have tried to simply duck the issue of her *Review* affiliation or to explain it away. For instance, David Maraniss claims that Hillary did not take all the material seriously. He even accused Blumstein and Phelan of distorting the facts. Nevertheless, Maraniss conceded that Hillary had more than a fleeting association with the journal, describing her role as reviewing and critiquing articles before they were published. Maraniss was right in suggesting Hillary's primary motivation was not ideological. At Yale Law School, an association with a radical journal brought visibility on campus and the approval of her professors.

Others have claimed that Hillary's flirtation with revolutionary politics has been exaggerated or that it was an aberration. A year later, however, after completing her second year at Yale, Hillary spent the summer of 1971 in Oakland as an intern in the law offices of Robert Treuhaft. A long-time member of the Communist Party USA, Treuhaft was extremely active in Bay Area activities of the party. His wife was the well-known British Communist, Jessica (Decca) Mitford.

Mitford is the author of *A Fine Old Conflict*, a memoir on the Communist party membership. Joan Smith, writing in the *San Francisco Examiner*, reviewed the book as "an inspired case for the bravery and effectiveness of (the Communist party's) members as they continued to espouse progressive causes when such liberal organizations as the ACLU and the NAACP were often intimidated into silence." According to Mitford, the book was her attempt to "lay to rest some myths created by the 'I was duped' school of American ex-party members."

Hillary was recommended to Treuhaft by some of her professors at Yale. She was looking for a "movement" law firm to work at for the summer. As it turns out, Hillary would continue her association and support of the Black Panther cause while working as a law clerk for Treuhaft. Treuhaft told Herb Caen of the *San Francisco Examiner*, "That was the time we were representing the Black Panthers, and she worked on that case. Some people think she went to Sacramento with them—remember when they disrupted the legislature?—but I'm not sure whether she did or not. Anyway, it was nice to have her around."

Like the Don Jones connection, however, the significance of Hillary's revolutionary phase has been misunderstood. Despite these affiliations, Hillary led a less-than-revolutionary existence.

Revealingly, Hillary remained an excellent student. Even as her colleagues railed about overthrowing the ruling class, she diligently prepared to become a part of it. Nor did anything in her personal life suggest deep alienation from the "system." In her second year, she shared a suite with Kwan Kwan Wang, who was from Burma. Wang told Donnie Radcliffe that Hillary was "very focused about her studies but she was easy to be around, down-to-earth, fun, endearing and caring. I call it Hillary's hippie stage when she wore big glasses and sloppy clothes." Classmate Carolyn Ellis agreed: "She looked like a hippie." Of course, at Yale Law School at this time, the hippie garb was a uniform. She didn't dress any differently than the majority of her classmates.

According to another classmate, "She did nothing to excess. She didn't do drugs. She was too cautious, and would never take such a risk. She took no joy in the illicit. The forbidden had no fascination for her—she lacked any self-damaging impulse."

In the spring of 1970, Hillary began her involvement with children's rights activists, another aspect of her life that would become controversial later. Through a bulletin board announcement, Hillary learned that Marian Wright Edelman would be speaking at Yale. Edelman headed the Washington Research Project, which would later become known as the Children's Defense Fund. Edelman's speech that day was the beginning of a long association. Hillary had read an article about Edelman and her work in *Time* magazine, and the two had briefly met at a League of Women Voters conference organized for young leaders by Edelman's husband, Peter, a former aide to Robert Kennedy. Hillary's picture in *Life* magazine had generated an invitation to the conference.

At the conclusion of Edelman's remarks, Hillary spoke with Edelman about her desire to somehow become involved in the Washington Research Project. With the summer of 1970 approaching, Hillary asked Edelman about the possibility of a job. Edelman explained that there was no money available for such a position. Hillary then volunteered to work as an intern, provided that she could obtain some type of funding to cover her expenses. Edelman readily agreed to take on an enthusiastic Yale law student who would cost her nothing. Hillary received a grant from Yale and spent the summer in Washington, D.C.

In Washington, Hillary was assigned to work with a Senate subcommittee that was chaired by then-Sen. Walter Mondale (D-MN), which was studying the conditions of migrant workers in labor camps. Her summer was spent interviewing migrant families in labor camps and recording their long list of everyday hardships.

During her second year of law school, Hillary continued to study law as it pertained to the family and the rights of children. She began to seek out courses and professors in this area, studying family law under Joseph Goldstein, a psychologist, and Jay Katz, a psychiatrist. Katz was assisted by Sigmund Freud's daughter, Anna Freud, who was a child psychologist and one of the founders of the Yale Child Study Center.

Although much has been written about Hillary at Yale, little attention has been paid to the fact that she stayed an extra year. And, she did so for the most old-fashioned of reasons. She had fallen in love.

During her second year at Yale, Hillary met Bill Clinton. A classmate who witnessed the events says that it was Hillary who pursued Bill, and she did so assiduously. According to the story that both Clintons repeat now, they first met in the law school library, a long narrow room. Bill was involved in a conversation at one end of the library while staring at Hillary, who was seated at the other end of the room studying. Hillary stood up, walked the length of the room, stood in Bill's face and declared, "Look, if you're going to keep staring at me, and I'm going to keep looking back, I think we ought to know each other's names. I'm Hillary Rodham. What's your name?"

Bill Clinton entered Yale Law School a year after Hillary. At this time he had long hair and a beard, and had spent two years in England as a Rhodes scholar. He was gregarious and popular and talked constantly about Arkansas. For Bill Clinton there was no question about what he was going to do after law school. He would return to Arkansas and seek a political career.

Arkansas, for those at Yale Law School, was known only as a place where hillbillies and racists lived. Hillary recalled in 1991, "Bill was always intent upon what he was going to do, which was come home to Arkansas. Most of us, including me when I first met him, didn't really have any idea of what that meant. I mean, we'd never been to Arkansas. We didn't know very much about the state." Alluding to the famous incident when the state's governor tried to stop integration of Little Rock's Central High School, she continued, "Frankly, what we knew was colored by 1957 and Orval Faubus. And so we just didn't really have much of an idea at all."

Bill and Hillary lived together in a house close to campus in New Haven during their final two years at

Yale in a small one-bedroom apartment. Clinton was forced to work several jobs to make ends meet. He had obtained a scholarship to attend Yale, yet it was not enough to cover his living expenses. The poverty of his youth that he spoke about during the 1992 presidential campaign is a myth, yet Clinton did not come from the kind of money that many of his classmates did. He held a wide range of jobs, which usually took precedence over class attendance. In the fall of 1970, Clinton worked on the U.S. Senate campaign of the anti-war candidate, Joe Duffy, who would lose in the election to Lowell Weicker. Bill taught a course at a local community college, worked on several other local political campaigns, and worked for a lawyer in downtown New Haven.

Bill and Hillary spent the summer of 1972 in Texas working on the presidential campaign of George McGovern. Clinton was one of two state coordinators. Bill and Hillary were devoted to the liberal McGovern. Co-worker Gary Mauro remembers that they would discuss nothing but the campaign. Everyone else would have a pitcher of beer in front of them, and they would order two Cokes.

Hillary's actual work in the campaign was registering new Hispanic voters for the Democratic party in San Antonio. Whereas Bill was a state coordinator, Hillary's job had far less rank. She worked under Sara Ehrman, a legislative aide from McGovern's Washington office. She recalls the first time she met Hillary, who was dressed in brown corduroy pants and a brown print shirt and had tied-back hair. Ehrman remembers her as a "smart, tough, determined kid."

Even in Texas in 1972, there was every indication that Clinton was seeing other women when Hillary was not around. David Maraniss wrote, "It was not at all certain during their Texas days that Rodham and Clinton would stay together. They did not see each other exclusively and appeared on the verge of splitting up at least once."

In November, Richard Nixon was elected in a landslide, capturing over 60 percent of the popular vote and 520 of 537 electoral votes. George McGovern carried only Massachusetts and Washington, D.C. Bill and Hillary returned to Yale after the election and passed all their final exams.

In 1973, her fourth year at Yale, Hillary helped research a book, *Beyond the Best Interests of the Child*. The book was written by Goldstein, Freud, and Albert Solnit, who was then director of the Yale Child Study Center. The book dealt with the rights of children in custody battles. It attempted to define standards for judges in cases involving parental custody. The standard proposed in the book was based on the assumption that "the least detrimental available alternative" should be applied in custody cases.

Hillary also did legal research for the Carnegie Council on Children after being recommended by Edelman. She helped research Kenneth Keniston's book, *All Our Children*. Specifically, she helped with the chapter that dealt with the legal protection of children. Keniston criticized *Beyond the Best Interests of the Child* as "a white paper giving parents unquestioned final authority over their children." He argued that children should have their own separate legal rights, a position postulated by Hillary in a 1973 article in the *Harvard Education Review* and in later law review articles in 1977 and 1979.

Upon graduation in 1973, Hillary went to work as a staff attorney for the Children's Defense Fund in Cambridge, Massachusetts. Bill Clinton turned down several opportunities in New York and Washington and returned to Arkansas. He had his sights set on a 1974 run for Congress against Republican John Paul Hammerschmidt in Arkansas' Third District.

According to Clinton, his initial plan was to set up his own law practice in his boyhood home of Hot Springs and run for Congress. Upon leaving Yale, however, Clinton claims he was driving home to Arkansas when he phoned Wylie Davis, the dean of the law school, and explained, "I don't have anything set to do; but I'm coming home to Arkansas, and you might want me to come teach up there because I'll teach anything, and I don't mind working, and I don't believe in tenure, so you can get rid of me anytime you want."

This story told by Clinton is a complete fairy tale. In fact, Clinton had been working on contacts in Fayetteville during his entire third year at Yale. He went to Fayetteville in May of that year for a very formal interview process, appearing before the Faculty Appointments Committee. Years later, when Davis heard Clinton's tale of a roadside phone call, he would amusingly ask, "Why ruin a Horatio Alger-type story with a self-inflicted nuisance like the facts?"

More important than the interview process was the intervention of Sen. J. William Fulbright, Clinton's mentor and a former president of the university. It was Fulbright who was responsible for getting Clinton the position. According to a university faculty member, "Fulbright made one call and Clinton got the job. It was no secret to anyone, least of all Fulbright, that Clinton was going to Fayetteville to run against Hammerschmidt."

In the fall of 1973, while he was in Fayetteville laying the foundation for his congressional campaign, Clinton was contacted by John Doar to work as his special assistant on the U.S. House of Representative's Judiciary Committee Impeachment Inquiry Staff. This committee was to lead the inquiry into the impeachment of Richard Nixon. Doar, former head of the Justice Department's Civil Rights Division under Presidents Kennedy and Johnson, was hired as the special counsel to lead the investigation. He needed a small staff of young lawyers who were not afraid of long hours, sometimes menial tasks, and tedious, exacting legal work. Clinton had been recommended to Doar by Burke Marshall. What better place to find young lawyers dedicated to the task of impeaching Nixon than Yale Law School?

Clinton turned down the opportunity, but recommended Hillary, who readily accepted and headed for Washington. Her relationship with Clinton was already paying off. This was a big break, enabling her to become a part of history. "What a gift," Hillary told Donnie Radcliffe. "I felt like I was walking around with my mouth open all the time."

Doar had, in fact, seen Bill and Hillary before. The two had competed in a mock trial competition with members of Yale's Barrister's Union. Doar had been a judge for the competition. Although they did not win, Doar remembered Bill and Hillary. It is not known if he remembered them for the content of their presentation or for the gaudy orange outfit that was worn by Hillary during the competition.

The impeachment committee regularly worked between twelve and sixteen hours a day. During this time, Hillary lived with Sara Ehrman in a townhouse in southwest D.C. Hillary and Ehrman were friends from the McGovern campaign in Texas. Ehrman remembers Hillary during this time as being totally consumed, physically and mentally, with the work of the committee. She told the *Washington Post*, "I barely ever saw her, I just remember driving her at 7 a.m. to the Watergate committee offices in a converted hotel. We used to laugh about the absurdity of the life she was leading."

Doar's staff numbered about a hundred persons, including forty-three lawyers. Hillary was one of three female lawyers. "People just worked around the clock," Hillary said. "It was an unbelievable experience. The staff that was put together was so professional, experienced. They were some of the greatest lawyers I've ever worked with. I was just a fresh, young law school graduate, and I got to work with these people."

Hillary assisted in the establishment of procedural guidelines while working for the constitutional and legal research section of the impeachment committee. This type of grunt work was perfect for Hillary, who fancied herself a student of the law. The work was the basic, straightforward sort of research that appealed to the analytical Hillary. She was to make sure that all activities of the committee were consistent with the Constitution. Her supervisor, Joseph A. Woods, Jr., has described the job as less than glamorous.

Hillary also had the privilege of listening to the famous Watergate tapes. She told the *Arkansas Gazette*, "I was kind of locked in this soundproof room with these big headphones on, listening to a tape. It was Nixon taping himself listening to the tapes, making up his defenses to what he heard on the tapes. . . . It was surreal, unbelievable, but it was a real positive experience because the system worked. It was done in a very professional, careful way."

Dagmar Hamilton, a lawyer on the committee from Texas, was impressed with Hillary's resourcefulness. Donnie Radcliffe explains how Hamilton was overwhelmed with Hillary's ability to make a chart. The two were asked "to find out about procedures." Hillary, to the apparent amazement of Hamilton, made a chart. Obviously, by the tone of Hamilton's praise, this was not as simple a thing as one might imagine. "It was done in a very lawyerly fashion. It showed initiative and her bright and analytical mind. I admired it. It was one of those good things that you look at and say, 'I wish I'd thought of that.' "

One of her superiors on the committee was Bernard Nussbaum, to whom she would years later award a job as White House counsel. Nussbaum, an expert on corporate takeovers who made a fortune during the "Decade of Greed" in the 1980s, would be forced from office after interfering in the Whitewater investigation. Nussbaum gave Hillary rides home to Ehrman's apartment after the long work days, "so the kid wouldn't get attacked."

Hillary talked incessantly about her boyfriend, Bill Clinton, who was running for Congress back in Arkansas. The work of the impeachment committee was exciting, but she knew her future was with Bill Clinton. She kept in close touch with the campaign and was known to pick up the phone and bark orders to whoever answered. There was also reason for her to worry about her relationship with Clinton. While she boasted of her boyfriend to colleagues, there is every indication that she was aware of his antics in the Ozarks. She even sent her father and brother Tony to Fayetteville, supposedly to help with the campaign. Others saw their presence differently.

David Maraniss wrote,

> There was another aspect to the presence of Hillary's father and brother in Fayetteville while she was still in Washington. One of the worst-kept secrets at headquarters was that Clinton had become involved in an intense relationship with a young woman volunteer who was a student at the university. . . . Aside from the Fayetteville woman, the staff also knew that Clinton had girlfriends in several towns around the district and in Little Rock. Perhaps they could disregard his rambunctious private life, but could Hillary? There was some suspicion that one of the reasons she sent the men in her family to Arkansas was to put a check on her boyfriend's activities.

On 9 August 1974, Nixon resigned. Gerald Ford became president, and the work of the impeachment committee was over. Hillary's job was done. Her future was with Bill Clinton, and it was time to go to Arkansas.

Hillary was the adoring wife during Bill Clinton's 1982 "comeback" gubernatorial campaign.

(Photo provided by *Arkansas Democrat-Gazette*)

Four

"Land of Opportunity"

Hillary Rodham Clinton became First Lady of the United States by way of Arkansas, and her ascent must be understood in light of the opportunities provided by such a place.

In the twenties, satirist H.L. Mencken wrote, "I know New Yorkers who have been to Cochin China, Kafristan, Paraguay, Somaliland and West Virginia, but not one who has ever penetrated the miasmic jungles of Arkansas."

In the years following World War II, a concerted effort was made by business and political leaders to promote the state as "The Land of Opportunity." Just as the state's image was turning the corner, the nation's attention would focus on the 1957 integration crisis at Little Rock's Central High School. Gov. Orval Faubus became famous as a defender of segregation. Images of young black children being escorted through mobs of jeering white citizens became etched indelibly in the psyche of the nation.

Baby boomers too young to remember the integration crisis did not escape Dogpatch imagery, either. During the mid-seventies, the hard rock band Black Oak Arkansas was a mild national success with its brand of hillbilly metal. When at its schlocky best, lead singer James "Jim Dandy" Mangrum, with whiskey jug close by, would prance around the stage shirtless, whacking on a wash-

board. Among the Black Oak originals was a song entitled "When Electricity Came to Arkansas."

Try as they might, political and business leaders in
Arkansas have never been able to shake the backward
image of their state. Hillary Rodham venturing to such
a place made no sense to anyone, except perhaps Bill
Clinton. For her, "The Land of Opportunity" had a
meaning all its own.

In August of 1974 Hillary joined Clinton at the University of Arkansas in Fayetteville. While most of Hillary's
Wellesley and Yale classmates were in New York, Washington, and Chicago, Hillary now found herself in
Fayetteville, tucked away in the northwest corner of the
state in the Ozark Mountains. To get to Fayetteville, one
must travel the Pig Trail, a winding road through the
Ozarks. Lou Holtz, the famous Notre Dame football coach,
was head coach at the University of Arkansas from 1977-
1983, and once commented, "Fayetteville is not the end
of the earth, but you can certainly see it from there."

Hillary had visited Arkansas the year before in 1973.
Bill Clinton had given her the grand tour. Rather than
driving straight from the airport to Hot Springs, Bill
decided on an eight-hour detour to show Hillary his state.
Hillary told *Newsweek*, "He took me to all these places he
thought were beautiful. We went to all the state parks.
We went to all the overlooks. And then we'd stop at his
favorite barbecue place. Then we'd go down the road
and stop at his favorite fried-pie place. My head was
reeling because I didn't know what I was going to see or
what I was expecting." Hillary was less than impressed
with the place, but she did take and pass the bar exam
in Arkansas on that visit in 1973.

While contemplating her move to Arkansas, Hillary
would rhetorically ask Washington friends, "Have you
ever been to Arkansas?" as if it was about the last place
on earth Hillary wanted to go. Hillary's Washington roommate, Sara Ehrman, reflected the feelings of most of
Hillary's enlightened friends who considered Arkansas

beneath them. She told the *Washington Post*, "I told her every twenty minutes that she was crazy to bury herself in Fayetteville. You are crazy. You are out of your mind. You're going to this rural remote place—and wind up married to some country lawyer." Wellesley friend Jan Piercy echoed the same. "People heard that Hillary was moving to Arkansas and couldn't believe it." Even Dorothy Rodham had doubts about her daughter's decision: "I wondered if Arkansas would be so great for Hillary, but you know, I've never told my children what to do. I had to rely on Hillary's judgment—there'd never been any reason not to."

"I kept struggling between my head and my heart," Hillary told Gail Sheehy in *Vanity Fair*. "Head said gold-plated law firm in New York or Washington, public-interest law, or government. Heart won." Hillary considered it a "leap of faith" when she moved to Arkansas. "I just knew I wanted to be part of changing the world, Bill's desire to be in public life was more specific than my desire to do good."

Yet, in choosing Arkansas, it can well be argued that Hillary was, in fact, following her head just as much as the proclaimed devotion to her heart. She must have been able to realize Clinton's political potential in Arkansas. After all, everyone else did. Bill Clinton had no intention of becoming a lawyer, much less a "country lawyer." The political landscape of the Ozarks was far different from Chicago, New York, or Washington. In that respect, Hillary must have seen the opportunity that Clinton did indeed have before him in his home state. Bill Clinton's Arkansas took on a whole new significance for Hillary's career plans. She certainly was not going to Fayetteville to become a tenured academic.

What had to be appealing to Hillary was that Arkansas was a one-party state. The Democratic party, or what is better known in Arkansas as the Democratic Machine, controlled politics. As Hillary's close friend Diane Blair explains in her book, *Arkansas Politics and Government*,

"The attachment of Arkansas voters to the Democratic party (and their negative view of Republicans) has been unsurpassed by voters in any other state. In proof of this assertion, one public opinion survey of Arkansas voters in 1958 found that the single most negative concept in the state was the concept of Republicanism."

Amazingly, there has never been a Republican elected to the United States Senate from Arkansas. When Hillary went to Arkansas in 1974, John Paul Hammerschmidt was the only Republican to have ever been elected to the U.S. Congress. At that time, there had been only one Republican governor in the state's history, Winthrop Rockefeller. With his money and the help of a skilled political organizer named Everett Ham, Rockefeller was elected governor in 1966 and reelected in 1968.

If Bill Clinton was going to enter politics, what better place to do so than in his home state, which also happened to be a small, one-party state. As Diane Blair has noted, in Arkansas you don't have to get in line and wait your turn. Clinton could immediately make the congressional race and then run for attorney general.

Hillary told Bill Clinton biographer Charles Allen about arriving in Fayetteville in 1974. "Bill was at that time (running for Congress). We had a very interesting first couple of months there, and I loved Fayetteville. I loved the university. I loved the law school. I loved my colleagues. I made some of the best friends I ever had in my life. It was an adjustment, in the sense that I'd never really lived in the South and I'd never lived in a small town, but I felt so immediately at home." It should be noted that Hillary made these remarks in February 1991, at a time when she was First Lady of Arkansas and her husband had, in all likelihood, already decided to run for president. A close friend of Bill and Hillary's at the time remembers her as being sincerely concerned with her teaching duties, but also as being distant and not at all comfortable in her new surroundings. This person remembers Hillary as aloof and extremely wary of the people around her.

Hillary's avowed love affair with Fayetteville notwithstanding, it is difficult to imagine that Hillary would immediately "fit right in." She had been living for the past four years in the world of left-wing activism in New Haven and Washington, not to mention her four years at Wellesley. Her work in Washington on the impeachment of Nixon had been demanding, but at the same time, it had put her in the midst of the national political scene. Fayetteville had to be a culture shock for her. Nothing she had experienced in Park Ridge, Wellesley, New Haven, or Washington could have prepared her for life in a small southern city.

In Norman King's biographical tribute to Hillary, *Hillary: Her True Story*, King cites an incident that occurred in Fayetteville during Bill's first term as governor in 1979.

> One anecdote that circulated was enough to draw a picture of someone who seemed to be inhabiting an alien planet peopled with far lesser humans than she was accustomed to. The setting was the football field at the University of Arkansas, where the Razorbacks were playing an exciting game. Screams of "Soo-ee, soo-ee! Oink, oink, oink!" filled the air. The governor was in his special box, waving his arms, standing, shouting, then sitting down again, overcome with emotion. The cheerleaders were cheering; the fans were howling. Chaos. Hillary was seated next to the governor. She was holding something in her hands. Oblivious to the excitement surrounding her, she was reading a book.

Hillary's first few months in Arkansas were consumed by Bill's congressional campaign. He was running against John Paul Hammerschmidt in Arkansas' Third Congressional District, a large district covering most of north and west Arkansas. Hammerschmidt had been elected in 1966 and had not had a difficult race since. Hammerschmidt was a businessman from Harrison, Arkansas, who had built a reputation as a person who could serve the interests of the business community, while at the same time, catering to the rest of his constituency.

Bill Clinton won 44 percent of the vote against three challengers in the Democratic primary. His opponents were State Sen. W.E. "Gene" Rainwater of Ft. Smith, Greenland Mayor James A. Scanlon, and Danville lawyer David Stewart. Clinton likes to tell people, "The only reason I ran for Congress is they couldn't get anybody else to do it." Nothing could be further from the truth. John Robert Starr wrote,

> Democrats, after ceding the Third District to Hammerschmidt in a couple of elections, decided to try to oust him in 1974. The man they expected to do it with was Rainwater, a popular state senator from Ft. Smith, the largest city in the district. However, other Democrats were not willing to cede the primary. . . . Clinton simply outworked the other three. He led the differential primary ticket by more than twenty-three thousand votes and demolished Rainwater in the runoff.

Clinton captured 69 percent of the vote in the runoff.

It was the classic battle of ideologies—the young liberal against the conservative Hammerschmidt. Clinton campaigned against Hammerschmidt's support of Richard Nixon and the Vietnam War. "No man who has stood in Congress and supported Nixon's policies, no man who has supported Nixon's vetoes, no man who tends to cover up the Watergate affair, deserves to represent this district," Clinton would bellow. He was sticking strictly to the script of anti-Republicanism that swept the country as a result of Nixon and Watergate.

Upon Hillary's arrival in Arkansas, she became Bill's unofficial campaign manager. She took charge of the campaign office and staff. The campaign had been a disorganized effort, dominated by Clinton's boisterous and overly active presence, until Hillary showed up. Those that were close to the campaign at the time can remember the first indications of Clinton's now well-known temper. Clinton was in many ways out of control during this campaign. His often childish behavior might be explained by the fact that he was only twenty-seven at the time.

According to a Fayetteville lawyer who was close to the campaign, Hillary's presence was not at all welcome by other campaign workers: "They hated her." Hillary created a tremendous amount of conflict among those who had worked diligently on the campaign from the start. Clinton's Fayetteville friend, Ron Addington, was one of the most dedicated. "Our organization went to sh——," recalled Addington. "We lost the spirit because of her. Everybody started bickering with everybody else." Hillary's condescending attitude created friction, especially among the female contingent of the campaign who were devoted to Bill Clinton. David Maraniss wrote, "After sending Clinton's University of Arkansas girlfriend into exile (the young woman was not seen around the campaign from October through election day), Rodham took on several aides whose style she disapproved of." Hillary's style was forward, vocal, and opinionated. She considered Fayetteville and her comrades on the campaign to be politically unsophisticated, and let those around her know it.

Joseph Merriweather, writing in 1990 for the *Arkansas Gazette*, a paper that rarely said a bad word about either of the Clintons, heard the same grumblings from campaign workers over the years. "Hillary Clinton has earned a reputation as demanding and impatient and, in the heat of political battle, she has been described as pushy, cold and domineering."

She also went after Clinton. The two would engage in loud and vulgar arguments in front of other campaign workers. Ron Addington told Maraniss, "They'd have the

biggest d——n fights, shouting and swearing. They had
two or three battle royals." These outbursts were very
much a part of the relationship. Fellow workers from the
McGovern campaign in Texas remember equally brutal
exchanges between the two.

Her whole family would eventually join in the effort.
Her father Hugh and brother Tony, who had spent the
summer in Arkansas keeping an eye on Bill and con-
structing yard signs, were joined by Dorothy and Hugh,
Jr. The participation of the Rodhams of Park Ridge in
the campaign provided for some irony. It is hard to
imagine Hugh Rodham, an affluent Republican Chicago
businessman, selling Bill Clinton to Democratic voters in
the Ozark Mountains.

Hillary did not make many public appearances with
Bill during that first campaign. That was not her role in
1974. The two, after all, were not yet married. Another
reason for her limited visibility in the campaign was her
physical appearance and attire. Hillary still dressed as
though she was at a peace rally on the quad at Yale. She
is remembered as an "eye-sore" by a friend of Bill
Clinton's who worked on the campaign. Former Arkansas Supreme Court Judge Jim Johnson remembers the
first time that he met Hillary. He remembers speaking
on the same platform with Bill during the campaign at
an event in Springdale, a town near Fayetteville. "The
first time I saw her she was in the hippy costume, with
heavy shell glasses. I remember introducing her incor-
rectly as Miss Rodman, rather than Rodham. She was
extremely gracious about it and was cordial, friendly and
as sweet as could be."

Hillary's abrasiveness had obviously been left at campaign headquarters, but as Johnson points out, the image of Hillary in Arkansas was that of a hippy. Clinton
himself was trying to shake that tag in conservative northwest Arkansas, and he did not need a flower child making public appearances with him. This is not a minor
point or one that is unfair to Hillary. In characterizing

her during this time, most people will mention her appearance before anything else.

The Democratic landslide that took place across the country was not enough to defeat Hammerschmidt. He won the race with 51.5 percent of the vote. Hammerschmidt would remain in Congress until 1992, and his victory over Clinton was the closest race of his career. As a result, Clinton had made quite a name for himself. It was obvious that this would not be his last campaign.

After the 1974 campaign, Bill and Hillary settled into their respective faculty positions. Bill related to the students more easily than Hillary. He was an easy grader, who did as much teaching in the student lounge as he did in the classroom. He was widely known for his procrastination with regard to grading papers and the posting of grades.

Hillary had arrived at the law school with much aplomb. Yale Law School and Watergate were not the only reasons for the curiosity. Her most noted credential was that she was Bill Clinton's girlfriend. Woody Bassett, a former student of Bill and Hillary's and a long-time Clinton supporter, remembers, "It was Hillary Rodham whom I remember the best from that year. On my first day in law school that fall, I took a seat in the criminal law class, and in strode Hillary Rodham, looking, I thought, a little out of place. She neither dressed or talked like she was from Arkansas. What a culture shock it must have been for her. All of us had heard a little about her. She was Bill Clinton's girlfriend."

As a teacher, Hillary more closely resembled her old teacher, Elisabeth King, the dour woman who had taught Hillary in grammar and middle school. She was considerably more demanding of her students than Bill.

Hillary taught criminal law and criminal procedures, as well as a seminar in children's rights. In student evaluations, Hillary was constantly chided for her appearance. Her habit of wearing no make-up, big Gloria Steinem glasses, and sloppy clothes appalled her students. According to Diane Blair, a fellow teacher, "Students would write things like, 'Please stop wearing those big old granny sweaters.' " Her midwestern accent, hippy clothes, and Eastern credentials together with a feminist chip on her shoulder kept her at arm's length from the students. The contrast between Bill and Hillary was striking. While Bill was comfortable talking Razorback football in the student lounge, Hillary was more at home in the law library researching some obscure aspect of the law. Students must have been baffled by Clinton's interest in the serious, ill-kept Hillary.

Yet, some friends of the two saw things differently. They did not openly live together as they had at Yale. Ever the politicians, they took into account the social standards of the time in the small southern city. But, it was well known that they spent a great deal of time together, regardless of their addresses. Hillary was sharing a house with her brother Hugh, who had stayed on after the campaign. He had previously spent two years in Colombia for the Peace Corps and was now taking classes at the university. Tony Rodham would eventually find his way to Fayetteville as well.

A person who worked at the university at the time and knew both Bill and Hillary remembers an arrogant Hillary who didn't have much time for those who could not, in some way, help her or Bill's career. "She was very selective. Her only real friends were Diane Blair and Ann Henry. She seemed to think that they were the only ones around here good enough for her—Ann's husband was the local Democratic chairman, Diane was originally from the East." This comment on Hillary's attitude towards people in Fayetteville is consistent with those of others who have observed Hillary over the years. In a 1994 article written by Connie Bruck in *The New Yorker*, an unnamed source is quoted as saying, "I think she has assigned a usefulness quotient to everyone in her life: Whom do I need to accomplish this? Everyone is part of a team to get from this point to the finished product. She's very political: Are you wealthy? Are you powerful? Have you written a book I like? Are you a star?"

Diane Blair was Hillary's closest friend in Fayetteville. The self-proclaimed feminist found a soul mate in Hillary. "Both she and I had been raised and educated outside the South and were more accustomed to big-city anonymity than to small town familiarity. Furthermore, we were both politically aware and active, anxious to advance the status of women. . . . It was not easy being a feminist in Arkansas in the 1970s, and Hillary and I were very glad to have each other for advice, comfort and comic relief."

Hillary's friends outside of Arkansas were still disappointed with her for giving up a career to be with Clinton in Arkansas. Why on earth would she go to a poor, racist place like Arkansas? One of her mentors, Peter Edelman, told her that when she went to Arkansas to be with Bill Clinton, she was throwing her life away. It was obvious that Bill, for whatever reasons, wanted to marry Hillary. He had paved the way for her to get to Arkansas. He had asked Hillary to marry him that first year in Fayetteville, but she had declined. She had many doubts about committing herself to a life in Arkansas, a place where she had few friends and was clearly uncomfortable. Hillary needed more time to see what Clinton could make of himself.

Hillary's decision to marry Bill would have been immediate if he had beaten Hammerschmidt. Bill's election would have meant a life in Washington and a quick departure from the state. Donnie Radcliffe explains: "Were Bill Clinton to win his congressional race, Hillary's dilemma about going to Arkansas would be solved because he would come to Washington. Of course then she would have a second dilemma, that of the congressional wife." This second dilemma would have been far more welcome for Hillary.

There was no doubt in anyone's mind that Bill would be running for office again. He had come home for a reason. He had never shown a real interest in practicing law. Teaching for Clinton was not a career goal, but rather a convenient and prestigious profession, which suited his need to campaign.

Hillary was still unsure about what to do with her life. After a year in Arkansas, the two were still not married, and it was well known that the only reason she was there was to be with Clinton. Yet, she had her own career to think about. She had not gone to Wellesley and Yale to become a teacher or simply a wife. She was not sure if there was enough in Arkansas to satisfy her professional desires. It had to be abundantly clear to her that she had no hope of a political career of her own in Arkansas. The same qualities that separated her from the students at the law school made her virtually unelectable in Arkansas. The internal dilemma for Hillary might have come down to one question. How far could Bill go?

The role that love played in the marriage of Bill and Hillary is debated by many in Arkansas. A startling number of people today view the marriage simply as a political arrangement. Hillary's ambition for power and influence is accepted as her primary motivation in her decision to marry Clinton. According to Diane Blair, right up to her wedding day, Hillary had doubts about whether she was doing the right thing.

Yet, when it came right down to it, Hillary bought into the promise of Bill Clinton's dreams. She believed in Clinton as a politician. It was not a stretch to see Clinton as governor or as a United States senator. Clinton's Yale roommate, Bill Coleman, has written:

> Had Bill Clinton at the age of twenty-five been a son of California, New York, Pennsylvania, or Illinois, the notion of successfully running for the United States Senate or a governorship would have appeared a bit far-fetched without far more politi-

cal seasoning because the political landscape in
those states was dominated by names like Dirksen,
Scranton, and Javits. . . . There was also an intui-
tive feeling that a small state that had every reason
to be proud of such a promising young man would
also forgive the mistakes and missteps that would
inevitably arise from idealism and youth.
Thus . . . the articulation of political ambitions directed toward an accessible home base amounted
to a nice fit rather than being the ravings of a
twenty-five-year-old egomaniac.

Clinton believed in himself more than anything in
the world. He sold Hillary on Bill Clinton, the politician.
It is unlikely that they were honestly thinking of the
presidency, but the ego of Bill Clinton is something never
to be underestimated. This is a person who, at the age of
twenty-four, with people his age dying in Vietnam, had
the nerve to write about his "political viability" after
dodging the draft.

Betsey Wright, the Clintons' closest adviser through
the 1980s, believes that they were thinking about the
presidency. According to Wright, Hillary thought that
Bill had the potential to be president, and it was very
much a part of her decision to marry him. In an interview with journalist Connie Bruck, Wright claimed Hillary
"saw that in him. . . . I'm not saying that's why she married him—but it was something she saw. And she's always
seen she could have political power with him—just not
elected. It was my shortsightedness that I felt when she
married him that she was giving up her chance for political power."

No doubt, another important issue for Hillary was
Bill's womanizing. It would be a mistake to believe that
Hillary did not know a great deal about Bill's sexual
activities outside of their relationship. As Hillary is constantly praised for her intelligence, it would be difficult
to believe that she was unaware of this side of Bill Clinton.

A person who attended Bill and Hillary's wedding reception recalls that Hillary was not in the dark at all and that Bill's womanizing "wasn't a maybe."

Hillary expressed her concern directly to her friends: "I know he's a womanizer, there's nothing that I can do about that. Can I live knowing that there will always be other women?" What might strike many people as remarkable is Hillary's possible tolerance of such an arrangement at this early date. It can be reasoned that Hillary hoped that Bill's shenanigans would eventually cease, considering the scrutiny to which politicians are subjected. She knew that above all else, the only thing that Bill Clinton truly ever cared about was his political viability. Based on that, perhaps she held out hope that Bill might some day stop.

As Bill and Hillary have admitted, the problem did not go away. When the two went on "60 Minutes" to talk about Bill's infidelity, the nation witnessed just how steeled Hillary had become on this issue. Kim Hendron, a Gravette, Arkansas, businessman and former state senator, echoed the feeling of many in Arkansas after hearing Clinton on tapes played by Gennifer Flowers: "I don't know many women that would listen to their husband on a tape like that, and still be with him." When it threatened Bill's candidacy, it was Hillary who insisted they confront the issue head on. Those who know the Clintons were hardly surprised. Hillary has been confronting the issue since the time the two had met at Yale.

In the summer of 1975, after a full year in Arkansas, Hillary needed some time away. She took a trip to visit her parents in Park Ridge and then traveled to New York, Boston, and Washington to check up on her friends and see what she had been missing. To her surprise, the visit with friends made her realize that life in the Ozark Mountains was not so bad after all. Bill definitely had a promising future there, and she wanted to be part of it. She told *Vanity Fair,* "I didn't see anything out there that

I thought was more exciting or challenging than what I had in front of me."

Upon her return to Arkansas, Bill again asked her to marry him. After picking Hillary up at the airport in Little Rock, Bill turned to Hillary in the car and asked, "You know that house you liked?" Hillary's response was, "What house?" He then reminded her of a small painted brick house near campus that she had commented on one day in passing. "Bill, that's all I said," responded Hillary. "I've never been inside it. What's all this got to do with us?"

"I'll tell you what it's got to do with us. I bought it," Clinton responded. "So I guess we'll have to get married now."

On Saturday, 11 October 1975, Bill Clinton and Hillary Rodham were married. Hillary was twenty-seven, Bill twenty-nine. The pastor's name, believe it or not, was Nixon. Victor Nixon was the pastor of the First Methodist Church and would later give the invocation before Clinton's acceptance speech at the 1992 Democratic National Convention in New York. Although Clinton was a Southern Baptist, he gave in to Hillary's demands to be married by a Methodist. This was no big deal for Clinton. At this time, he was not a churchgoer. He did not attend church regularly until he was defeated by Frank White for governor in 1980 and realized that it was politically advantageous to do so.

Reverend Nixon remembers Bill contacting him in August to see if he was willing to marry them. He was glad to oblige the couple and told Clinton that he'd like to sit down and discuss the marriage with them at some point. "And (Bill) asked what the visit would be about. He said, 'Well are you going to ask us questions?' And I said, 'Well I don't know. I may ask some.' I think Hillary wanted to know what the questions were so she could study for the visit."

Bill and Hillary were not married in a church. The wedding was a very small affair in the house Clinton had bought on California Avenue. Only immediate family members were present. Hillary's parents made the trip down a week prior to the ceremony to get the house in shape for the wedding. Dorothy also had to help her daughter get a wedding dress. She had a justifiable concern given Hillary's dressing habits. The wedding dress was bought off the rack at Dillard's, a Fayetteville department store, the day before the wedding.

Hillary retained her maiden name. She said that it was important to have her own identity, although she would quickly shed it a few years later. Over the years, the maiden name retention coupled with the fact that they were not married in a church would lead many in the state to mistakenly question the validity of the marriage.

The wedding reception took place later that day with over two hundred friends and political allies attending. It was held at the home of their close friends, Ann and Morris Henry. Morris Henry was the local Democratic chairman. Ann Henry was one of Hillary's few close friends in Fayetteville. Clinton turned the day into a political event. He announced that he would be running for office in 1976, either for attorney general, or possibly, another attempt to unseat Hammerschmidt. Every prominent politician and political contributor from the area was invited to the reception.

Interestingly enough, Jim Guy Tucker, the Arkansas attorney general, was present at the function. He had his sights set on a run for Congress, thus creating the possibility of Clinton running for attorney general in 1976. This reception was important for Bill Clinton because it was proof of the solid political base he had built up during the two years since leaving Yale. As evidenced by his guest list, Clinton was ready for his next race.

Bill's mother, Virginia, would never really get along with Hillary. At this point, Virginia was distraught over her new daughter-in-law. She was brought to tears when she learned that Hillary would not be taking Clinton's name. She considered it some "Yankee" thing. In her autobiography, *Leading With My Heart: My Life*, she describes a long-standing rocky relationship with Hillary. On her first meeting with Hillary, she "didn't know what to think. . . . No makeup. Coke bottle glasses. Brown hair with no apparent style. Even though Roger and I were polite, I guess our expressions gave us away, because the minute Hillary went to her bedroom to unpack her bag, Bill shot us a withering look." Virginia went on to write that she and Roger "wished [Hillary] would hop the next plane out."

Hillary remembers their first meeting much the same way. "When I first met her she thought I was from outer space, and I thought she was from outer space . . . and we looked at each other like, 'Who is this?' "

Virginia wrote, "Bill may be appalled to read this, though I think he understood what was happening better than Hillary or I did. I know he's told a friend, 'There was almost a kind of cultural tension between Mother and Hillary.' I guess that's as good a way to put it as any."

Bill and Hillary did not plan on taking a honeymoon. Dorothy convinced them to take a trip and, ultimately, the whole family decided to take a honeymoon together. Hillary's parents and brothers joined Bill and Hillary on a ten-day trip to Acapulco. Hillary's brother Hugh told *People* magazine, "Bill and Hillary didn't have time to take a real honeymoon, and then my mom came up with the idea of going to Mexico. We got a special rate and all went down together." When Bill gave the eulogy at his father-in-law's funeral in 1993, he recounted how the "whole family" went to Acapulco for his honeymoon. While the Rodhams and their new son-in-law spent ten days on the beaches of Acapulco, Bill's mother, Virginia, and brother, Roger, drove back home down the Pig Trail to Hot Springs. The differences between these two families could not have been bigger.

While Hillary's family was a model of fifties stability, Bill's was a confusing series of marriages, relationships, tragedies, and births. Bill's father, a traveling salesman named William Jefferson Blythe III, was killed in a 1946 car crash before Bill was born. Although only twenty-four, his marriage to Virginia was his fourth. He conceived a child with his first wife after they were already divorced. His second marriage was to his first wife's sister, and it is unclear whether he legally divorced her before marrying his third wife, who gave birth eight days after the wedding. When Blythe married Virginia, he was not legally divorced from his third wife.

Virginia herself would be married five times to four different men and widowed three times. Early in life, Bill was raised by his grandparents, and then by Virginia and Roger Clinton, to whom Virginia was married twice. Bill took Clinton's name as a teen-ager in Hot Springs, Arkansas. The elder Clinton for years battled a drinking problem and died in 1967.

Virginia passed away on 6 January 1994, succumbing to breast cancer. The colorful Virginia was seventy years old. She was active to the end, having just returned from a New Year's trip to Las Vegas at the time of her death. The loss to Clinton was a painful one. There was no one more important, or supportive of him, in his life. The two were so close that Clinton would never object to anyone referring to him as a "mama's boy." The *Washington Post* reported on the day after her death, "Behind Virginia Kelley's exotic public persona was a strong woman who more than anyone, even more than Hillary Rodham Clinton, shaped Bill Clinton."

Although many Park Ridge high-schoolers make it to elite Eastern colleges, very few from Arkansas do. Yet, Bill Clinton received an education every bit as outstanding as Hillary's. He attended Georgetown as an undergraduate and then went on to Oxford and Yale Law School. After getting his law degree, his immediate return to Arkansas to challenge Hammerschmidt confirmed his commitment to a political career. The academic credentials he earned outside the state never failed to impress, especially when it came to reporters and editors. He wielded his education as a political tool, never failing to mention his Rhodes Scholarship. But, he also realized that to the average voter he had to remain one of the "good ol' boys." For many people in the Ozarks, the only Oxford they had ever heard of was the one in Mississippi. When it serves his political purpose, Clinton has always loved to play the role of the country bumpkin, or Bubba. Even today, he plays it well and uses it to portray himself as a man of the people. Yet, the truth is that there is much about Bill Clinton that isn't very Arkansas.

One has to look no further than his wife. The value of Arkansas as a base for his political ambitions was never lost on Clinton, but at the same time he readily searched beyond its borders. The congressional campaign proved to be the first of many performances by Bill Clinton. It was also an affirmation of the duality of his life.

This duality finds its ultimate manifestation in his marriage to Hillary. Clinton brought Hillary back to Arkansas to be a part of his political ascent. Would Bill have gone to Washington out of love to be with Hillary had she not made the decision to join him in Fayetteville? All evidence suggests he would not have. As Clinton demonstrated by heading off to Georgetown, he always looked beyond Arkansas' borders, but always knew that it was his "Land of Opportunity." Hillary maintained the link between the two worlds. His relationship with Hillary was important because it kept him in touch with the important realm outside Arkansas, and the political opportunities it ultimately was to provide. Your typical Arkansas politician had gone to the University of Arkansas and married the Homecoming Queen. No matter how at home Bill was at Razorback Stadium, Hillary served as a reminder that he was not your average Arkansan.

Vince and Lisa Foster, Hillary and Bill Clinton, 1985.
(Photo provided by *Arkansas Democrat-Gazette*)

Five

The Hillary Problem

When he said it, a slight flush came to her face. The bottoms of her big round eyeglasses pushed against the pudge of her cheeks, making for a self-conscious, slightly goofy look. Bill Clinton was announcing he was running for attorney general, and since the job paid only six thousand dollars, he told reporters Hillary was to be the family's breadwinner. Previous attorney generals had practiced law privately while in office. He explained that he would not, enabling him to give full attention to the attorney general's position, which for Clinton meant full-time campaigning for governor.

The campaign for attorney general was kicked off on 16 March 1976. It was a race Bill Clinton knew he could easily win. As John Robert Starr described in his book entitled *Yellow Dogs and Dark Horses* on recent Arkansas political history,

> Clinton had the organization ready for a statewide campaign in 1976, but he had nowhere to use it until Jim Guy Tucker gave up the attorney general's office to run for Congress. Clinton didn't want to run again in the Third District. Hammerschmidt, no longer handicapped by association with a scandal-hounded president, had mended his local fences since 1974. There was no chance he would ignore Clinton this time. Clinton knew he would make an ideal candidate for attorney general. . . . Fortunately for Clinton, the temptation of going to Washing-

ton was too great for Tucker and he ran for Congress.

To Clinton, the governor's office was within sight. He would bide his time as attorney general for two years. In early 1976, Clinton took a leave of absence from his teaching position in Fayetteville. In May, Clinton won an easy primary victory. He collected 60 percent of the vote in a three-way primary. There was no Republican candidate. Clinton would take office in January of 1977.

Hillary was very much in the background during the campaign. It was a deliberate decision. In a race that was his to lose, Clinton did not want to answer questions about his odd-looking wife with a different last name. Hillary became only a minor issue in the campaign, which, for the most part, was devoid of any real debate. Asked by a reporter, "Will the fact that your wife has retained her maiden name hurt you politically?" Clinton responded simply, "I hope not." He explained briefly that Hillary "had made quite a name for herself as a lawyer" and was a "nationally recognized authority on children's rights." The issue resurfaced infrequently. The youthful Clinton was an energetic campaigner and did not suffer greatly from her absence from his side. Hillary's influence was exercised behind the scenes.

The couple took a vacation to Spain after Clinton's primary victory. It was there that Clinton was contacted by the Jimmy Carter presidential campaign and offered the job of coordinating Texas, a position similar to the one he had held in the McGovern campaign. Clinton declined. Rex Nelson explains, "Bill's decision not to take the Texas post was based partly on the attitude of Carter's volunteer staff in Arkansas—they were upset by the tendency of the national campaign headquarters to staff state offices with out-of-state workers. With his eyes on the governor's job even before he had taken office as attorney general, Bill knew he could not afford to alienate Arkansas Democrats." Never one to miss an opportunity, Clinton agreed to coordinate Carter's Arkansas campaign on a part-time basis. At the time, it was difficult to determine which race he was actually working on, Carter '76 or Clinton '78.

Despite his concern about the appearances of out-of-state coordinators, Clinton dispatched his wife to Indiana to work on the Carter campaign, one of the most Republican states in the nation. This continued the pattern of keeping Hillary "behind the scenes" early in his career. He was about to assume his first elective office and was laying the groundwork for his governor's bid. The party activists who worked on the Carter campaign were the same people he expected to work on his. The last thing he needed was Hillary alienating his future campaign workers.

Hillary left for Indiana in August of 1976. Indiana offered little hope for Carter. Hillary tried to put things in their best light: "I'm flattered they asked me to do it, especially since Indiana is supposed to be such a tough state." She worked under state coordinator Douglas Coulter, who spent most of his time traveling across the state. Hillary organized the campaign headquarters in Indianapolis and served as field coordinator in charge of volunteers in ninety-two counties. She quickly built a reputation as an effective organizer. Yet, the same abrasiveness known to those in the Arkansas campaigns quickly became apparent. William Geigreich worked with Hillary in Indiana. He told Donnie Radcliffe, "She didn't sugar-coat. You never had to wonder. If I said, 'How are we doing in such and such a county?' she'd say, 'You're a disaster. This is what people are telling me.' "

Ruth Hargraves, an Arkansan working on the Indiana campaign remembers that "[Hillary] could outargue anybody, and the last thing you wanted to do, particularly if it was at the end of the day and you were dead tired, was disagree with her. You always knew she was going to win."

The Carterites' efforts were all for naught, as President Ford captured Indiana with 53 percent of the vote. But, Hillary did make a favorable impression with Carter's victorious national team. She had paid her dues in a place that most knew was hopeless. A year later, in 1977, she would be rewarded for her efforts with an appointment to the board of the Legal Services Corporation, a large government-funded program to provide legal assistance to the poor.

In late 1976, Bill and Hillary sold their small house in Fayetteville and bought a new house in Little Rock. The life that Hillary had romanticized to friends was quickly forgotten.

On 1 February 1977, Hillary joined the "acquisitive and competitive corporate life" of which she had spoken so disparagingly in her Wellesley and Yale days. She went to work at the firm of Rose, Nash, Williamson, Carroll, Clay & Giroir, better known as the Rose Law Firm. For the Rose firm, the most powerful in the state, the decision to hire Hillary must not have been very difficult. Her Yale Law School credentials were impressive, and firms at this time were trying to hire more women. And, what better woman to hire than the wife of the state's attorney general, a man who was clearly on his way to becoming governor?

The Rose firm, founded in 1819, is one of the oldest law firms west of the Mississippi. Uriah M. Rose was a prominent attorney during the latter half of the nineteenth century. He was one of the founders of the American Bar Association, and a statue in his honor can be found in Statuary Hall at the U.S. Capitol. Over the years, the Rose firm has had six state Supreme Court justices drawn from its ranks and countless state legislators. As a result, the firm has tremendous clout and influence in the affairs of state and city governments. This cozy relationship was a profitable one for the firm. After her husband was elected governor, Hillary became not only the firm's first female partner, but also the youngest one ever as well.

Arkansans remember surprisingly little about Hillary during Clinton's term as attorney general. She lay low and pursued her new career. Her earnings at first were modest by the standards of blue chip firms in New York, but they provided a comfortable income for Little Rock. She made $24,250 in 1978. Bill, in fact, made more than Hillary that year. The attorney general's position had been made full-time, and he earned $26,500.

Hillary's law partner, Vincent Foster, explained to *The American Lawyer* that while Hillary "took domestic matters on it was not something that we were trying to encourage or promote at the law firm. So while she continued to do some family law quietly, she really was trying to build her commercial litigation practice." Most significantly, Hillary was exposed to the hand-and-glove relationship between Arkansas politics and big business, and the dazzling financial opportunities it provided for the well-connected.

The most profitable of these opportunities came from an unlikely source—a professional poker player named "Red" Bone. Hillary's dealings with Bone were so remarkable that they were kept hidden from the public for fifteen years. On 11 October 1979, three weeks before her husband was elected governor, Hillary invested one thousand dollars in cattle futures with Ray E. Friedman & Co. (REFCO) of Springdale, Arkansas. Ten months later, she cashed out with one hundred thousand dollars in profit.

Hillary was introduced to Red Bone and the REFCO office through her close friend Jim Blair, who worked as outside counsel for Tyson Foods, which is located in Springdale, Arkansas. Red Bone had worked for Tyson for thirteen years and was a close, personal friend of Don Tyson, head of the company. In 1977, Bone had been barred from trading by the Commodity Futures Trading Commission for manipulation of the egg market. Blair and Bone were close associates, Blair having represented Bone for two of his divorces. Tyson Foods was in the process of becoming the nation's largest supplier of poultry products and the state's largest employer. Don Tyson had supported Clinton in his race against Hammerschmidt and had contributed to Clinton's attorney general and gubernatorial campaigns. Tyson, Blair, and Bone might have figured out a way to make sure the young governor would stay a friend.

Hillary has given many different versions of her remarkable success in the cattle futures market. Her original version of events was that she made all the trades herself and did her own research by reading the *Wall Street Journal*. Because of the absurdity of her claim, however, she had to quickly acknowledge that her friend James Blair did most of the trades. She also advanced another explanation: "I was lucky." It is preposterous to believe that Hillary Rodham earned a 10,000 percent profit in the commodities market on her own, or for that matter, with guidance. Jack Hughes, a former Chicago Board of Trade pit trader, believes that "Hillary didn't actually trade that well, and neither did anyone else."

Commodities trading is a highly volatile, risky business; studies show that 75 percent to 90 percent of small traders end up losing money. Remarkably, her account made money on twenty-six out of thirty-one trades.

Experts have concluded that Hillary must have been the beneficiary of "allocated trades" when presented with the details of Hillary's amazing windfall. The practice is illegal. To put it simply, a trader such as Bone would make commodities trades, but not with specific account names or numbers. At the end of the day, Bone could then allocate winning trades to certain individuals, and losing trades to others. In December of 1979, Bone was disciplined by the Chicago Mercantile Board for "serious and repeated violations of record-keeping functions, order-entry procedures, margin requirements and hedge procedures."

For evidence that Hillary's account was special, one need look no further than the margin calls which Hillary never had to meet. In commodities, unlike stocks and bonds, investors can lose more than they invest. Brokers require clients to maintain a reserve or "margin" account, in order to cover a bad turn in the market. Hillary made $5,300 on her very first day in the cattle futures market off an initial investment of only $1,000. Experts say that she did not have enough money in her account to cover a trade that would result in such a profit.

That first $5,300 was peanuts compared to later trades. On 12 July 1979, the margin for cattle was $1,500 per contract and Hillary owned 65 contracts. She needed $97,500 in her account, which at the time was negative $20,000. In other words, the margin call from REFCO would have been $117,500 had it come. Needless to say, Hillary never got a margin call. According to *USA Today*, on the same day of 12 July, REFCO customer Stanley Greenwood's investments "were liquidated when he failed to post $48,000 to cover his losses."

"I cannot believe that REFCO would back her losses and cover her margin call," Gerald Celente, a former trader with REFCO told *Spy* magazine. "When I was dealing with them, they always demanded immediate payment for margins. I had to pay promptly, or else they could have closed my account. . . . Sure, had I been given the same treatment Hillary got, I would have cleaned up, too."

There is no question that Hillary's account was given special treatment. The real question in all this is where the money came from. Commodities trading is a zero sum game; in order for someone to make $100,000, someone had to lose that amount. The cattle futures market would clean out Blair, Bone, and most of the people trading through the Springdale REFCO office a short time after Hillary closed out her account in July of 1980. Hillary walked away with $100,000, while others lost millions.

The Little Rock Airport Commission named Hillary as its attorney in January 1978. This post was her first formal foray into the tangled web of Arkansas politics, and confirmed her newly acquired "insider" role. The commission was praised by the Little Rock chapter of the American Association of University Women for hiring a woman for the post. Commission member Seth Ward, father-in-law of Hillary's Rose Law Firm partner Web Hubbell, stated that "this was a chance for us to get a woman on the staff and involve women in the airport operations."

Clinton's two years as attorney general were unspectacular except for his tireless campaigning for the governor's office. When Clinton announced his candidacy for governor on 5 March 1978 at the Old State House in Little Rock, polls showed that in a five-man Democratic race he had the support of 57 percent of those surveyed.

This race was perfect for Clinton. Up against a weak field of career politicians and a turkey farmer, Clinton was able to exploit the media's affinity for his out-of-state education credentials and slick campaigning style. He raised close to five hundred thousand dollars for the primary race, which at that time was an unheard of amount of money for a political campaign. While the other four candidates used volunteers, Clinton had fifteen paid campaign workers. On 30 May 1978 Clinton captured the Democratic primary with 60 percent of the vote.

True to form, the Republican opposition in the general election was weak. The candidate was Lynne Lowe, a farmer and Republican state chairman from Texarkana. Clinton was swept into office with close to 65 percent of the vote in the general election. Thirty-two-year-old Bill Clinton became the nation's youngest governor.

Clinton was inaugurated on 10 January 1979. He was sworn in with a beaming Hillary at his side, along with his mother and brother Roger. The Clintons' inaugural ball was a garish affair themed "Diamonds and Denim."

Arkansas' Crater of Diamonds State Park is the only place in North America where diamonds can be found. The occasion was supposed to be a combination of sophistication and the down home. Blue jeans were as welcome as formal wear. Hillary was dressed in an embarrassing get-up, which was modeled after her wedding gown. Added to the basic design of the gown were pieces of other dresses worn by previous First Ladies. The sorry-looking gown today can be found in the Little Rock Old State House Museum. The designer of the gown, Connie Fails of Little Rock, has said that she wishes her creation could be buried.

Clinton created a minor controversy by inviting former governor Orval Faubus. Clinton was shrewd enough to know that Faubus, to many in Arkansas, represented the best of their populist past. To Hillary and her liberal friends, he represented nothing but Arkansas' segregationist past. Most were probably unaware that Faubus was elected by the people of Arkansas four times after the Central High School crisis of 1957 and still retained enough affection to have garnered 35 percent of the vote in the Democratic gubernatorial primary in a whimsical 1974 bid. The wariness might have been mutual, however. In a 1993 conversation, Faubus remembers her as "not arrogant, but somewhat aloof. I didn't meet her that night. I've been invited to the governor's mansion by Bill a few times since then. I've never had a conversation with her. She doesn't go out of her way to talk to people she isn't close to. Bill's different, you can't be in his presence without liking him."

The ascension of Clinton to the governor's mansion meant an end to Hillary's imposed anonymity. "I'm the First Lady, Bill's the First Man and Zeke's the First Dog," Hillary told the *Arkansas Gazette* in one of her first interviews of 1979. It was irreverent comments such as this that set the tone for Hillary's first disastrous tenure in the governor's mansion. She was as far from the traditional First Lady of Arkansas as one could get, and this was fine with the indignant Hillary. Hillary biographer Norman King writes in *Hillary: Her True Story*, "Still addicted to the style of the sixties—shapeless clothes and wildly disarranged hair—and wearing thick horn-rimmed glasses . . . Hillary Rodham was an anomaly as she entered the governor's mansion. She still insisted on being called Hillary Rodham, not Hillary Clinton. She was widely suspected, frowned upon, if not totally disliked, and kept at arm's length. . . . The public generally disliked her from the beginning."

Shortly after the election, Hillary was finally pinned down on the issue of her maiden name. As in the attorney general's race, the issue had been successfully kept out of the campaign. Her response did little to allay criticism or endear her to the public. "I had made speeches in the name of Hillary Rodham. I had taught law under that name. I was, after all, twenty-eight when I married, and I was fairly well established." Hillary told the *Arkansas Democrat* that keeping her maiden name made her feel like a "real person."

Frank White remembers that the issue of Hillary's name had been cleverly avoided by the Clinton campaign. "Most Arkansans didn't know that Hillary didn't have his name when they elected him. They knew her name was Hillary but they didn't know her name was Hillary Rodham. They thought she was Hillary Clinton. Well, she was very specific that she was Hillary Rodham after they were elected. I think it was a case of people not really knowing what they were getting."

Bill defended his wife in his best aw-shucks, down-home manner. Bill said,

> It depresses her some when she thinks it [the use of her maiden name] is hurting me, but she's a lawyer and she doesn't want to go into the courtroom as somebody's wife. If people knew how old-fashioned she was in every conceivable way, they probably wouldn't do that. She's just a hardworking, no-nonsense, no-frills, intelligent girl who has done

well, who doesn't see any sense to extramarital sex,
who doesn't care much for drink, who's witty sharp
but without being a stick in the mud. She's just
great.

For Hillary, Little Rock was a stepping stone to
Washington. She felt that she could call herself whatever
she wanted, and the people of the state would have to
understand. She wasn't going to change her name—they
would have to change their backward ways. The plan was
for Bill to serve three wildly successful terms, then take
on David Pryor in 1984, after which she would be headed
to Washington as the wife of a U.S. senator.

The "Hillary problem" was more than one of public
relations.

Clinton was defeated for reelection in 1980, and many
pointed to his ill-suited wife. It would be unfair to give
Hillary all the blame for the loss, but she represented all
that was wrong with the first Clinton administration.
Clinton's staff had become known as the "Bearded Wonders" for their long hair, out-of-state backgrounds, and
liberal politics. To many Arkansans, it seemed that the
"Bearded Wonders" had the attitude that they had come
to office to demonstrate to the poor, unworldly natives
how things should be.

As Gail Sheehy put it in *Vanity Fair*, "In 1978 the
Clintons swept into the Governor's office with the promise of youth and purity. 'Arrogant' was the outcry of the
Establishment, and the governor's spouse became the
lightning rod for people's resentment. To southerners
expecting a more decorative First Lady, Hillary Rodham
was an eyesore."

Clinton also managed to alienate many state workers
and officials. One staffer remembers being called into a
meeting in January 1979 to be advised that from that day
forward, any successes in the department were to be credited to Clinton. "We were told that when dealing with the
press we shouldn't personally take credit for anything.
Bill Clinton did everything. It was clear to us all that

from very early on he was running for the U.S. Senate. The attitude that he was on his way somewhere else and using us to get there resulted in him losing the support of most state employees. And I think this was a reflection of Hillary, that they were always going someplace else."

In September 1979, Hillary announced that she was pregnant. She and Bill had learned of her condition a few months earlier, but had kept the news to themselves. When she began to show physically, they decided to make the announcement. When the press inquired what the baby's last name would be, Hillary quickly responded, "Oh, it'll be Clinton."

Chelsea Victoria Clinton was born on 27 February 1980, the same date as Bill's father, W. J. Blythe. Bill had just returned to the governor's mansion from one of his frequent trips to Washington at 7:45 P.M. when Hillary went into labor. The baby was born at Little Rock's Baptist Medical Center and weighed six pounds, one and three-quarter ounces. She was born two weeks prematurely. Doctors were forced to perform a Caesarean section after four hours of painful labor. Hillary described Chelsea as her "one perfect child."

Diane Blair, Hillary's friend from Fayetteville, was present, and remembers Bill proudly walking around the hospital with Chelsea in his arms and acting "like he'd invented fatherhood." She remembers Clinton saying he was "bonding" with his new daughter. Bill was thrilled with Chelsea's arrival. Hillary stated years later, "I think for a long time, because his father died before he was born, Bill didn't believe he'd ever live to be a parent. That was something almost beyond his imagination." She told *Newsweek*, "He was amazed by fatherhood. He was overwhelmed by it. I've heard him say that when he saw his child, he realized it was more than his own father got to do."

The name Chelsea was Bill's choice. Bill and Hillary had visited England in the summer of 1979. "We were trying to have a child, something we were working on,"

Hillary told *Newsweek*. "And it was this glorious morning. We were going to brunch and we were walking through Chelsea, you know, the flower pots were out and everything. And Bill started singing 'It's a Chelsea morning.'" The Judy Collins song was one of Bill's favorites.

In order for Hillary to maintain her legal career and other outside interests, she had the Arkansas taxpayers provide her with a nanny for Chelsea, even though such a practice was against the law. One week after Chelsea's birth, Dessie Sanders was hired to care for the baby. Sanders was listed on payroll forms as a security guard in an attempt to hide a state-sanctioned baby sitter. The deception was uncovered by a newspaper in 1981, but the issue was ignored because Clinton had already been defeated. In a 1993 article in *The American Spectator*, Lisa Schiffren wrote, "Ignoring official job designations is common when hiring legitimate office staffers, but it makes sense in this case only if one assumes that the taxpayers should pay for a personal nurse for the governor's baby. In any case, nowhere on their 1980 tax return did either Yale trained lawyer/parent remember to list that $3,130 taxpayer gift as income."

Hillary took a four month leave of absence from the Rose firm after Chelsea's birth. As evidenced by her free nanny, Hillary's situation was not typical of the average working mother. Donnie Radcliffe wrote, "In the rarefied world of powerful elected officials where the perks included rent-free mansions staffed by full-time cooks, housekeepers, gardeners and security guards, Hillary was doubly blessed by belonging to a prestigious law firm that valued her association so much that she was encouraged to arrange her schedule to suit her personal needs." She spent the months of July and August splitting time between Rose and the governor's mansion, having work sent there from the office. As the wife of the governor, she could do as she pleased at the firm.

On a political level, Bill and Hillary expected to make the most of their new arrival, hoping that the birth of a child might make them appear more like a traditional couple. Whatever progress was made on this front was undone when Chelsea's birth was announced in Arkansas newspapers. It stated, "Governor Bill Clinton and Hillary Rodham had a daughter." Commenting on the wording of the announcement, Hillary later told the *Arkansas Times*, "I think that really disturbed people. It set up a kind of dissonance between me and other people and kept them from hearing anything else I might have to say."

When Bill Clinton lost to Republican Frank White in the 1980 general election, it was a shock to all. In the last week of the race, polls varied between twelve and eighteen points in Clinton's favor. Regardless of how bad Clinton's first term had been, it was unthinkable that the Republicans would actually capture the governorship.

White ran an effective campaign. He was not the normal sacrificial Republican candidate. A former Democrat and a graduate of the U.S. Naval Academy, White had been head of the state's industrial development corporation and was a successful Little Rock banker. He was able to criticize Clinton's lack of any experience in the "real world." White explained to Arkansans that they needed "mature leadership, someone with business experience, someone who has met a payroll and who has indicated by what they've said they will stop the uncontrolled growth in state government."

As Rex Nelson wrote in his 1993 book *The Hillary Factor*,

> Bill had an image problem. He and Hillary were increasingly viewed by many Arkansans as arrogant. Some never cottoned to Hillary's use of her maiden name. . . . Still, White could never have been elected if not for thousands of Arkansans who were so sure Clinton would win reelection that they decided to use their vote as a protest. They wanted to send a message to the arrogant young Democrat and his snooty wife.

Clinton did not call White after the defeat—a classless act. His concession speech did not come until the day after the election. A stunned gathering of his campaign workers joined Bill, Hillary, and Chelsea on the lawn of the governor's mansion. Reporter Jeff Katz remembers the scene at the governor's mansion that day. "It was like a wake. I've never seen so many people in tears. I've never seen so many dark glasses. Thank goodness it was a sunny day so they could disguise it but people were just incredibly shook up."

Bill, Hillary, and Chelsea moved out of the governor's mansion in January 1981 and into the affluent Hillcrest section of the city. The finest homes in Little Rock can be found in this neighborhood, which sits on a hill looking down, both geographically and figuratively, on the rest of the city. There was hardly any comfort to be found, however, in their new surroundings. The months following the defeat were difficult, tense times in the Clinton household. The former governor and his wife did not handle failure well. Judith Warner wrote, "Tempers in the Clinton household were flaring. . . . It was a troubled time. A period of soul searching, some might even say self-indulgence. For the next six months, friends say, Bill wasn't himself. He seemed aimless, depressed. For once he actually withdrew from people, preferring seclusion and introspection."

By most accounts Bill and Hillary were having serious problems in their marriage. The womanizing that Hillary was so familiar with was now becoming public. According to Judith Warner, "Bill Clinton sought absolution—and comfort—from anyone who would offer it. Many people have suggested that his infidelities started at this point. . . . Observers of Bill at this time agree that he did become, above all, very careless in his comportment."

Even Charles Allen, in his sympathetic book *The Comeback Kid*, acknowledged Clinton's extramarital activities at this time. "Clinton, seeing his political future vanish overnight, became careless about his actions. . . . Rumors began filtering into the newsrooms and throughout state offices that Clinton was having an affair with another woman. Such rumors about politicians are commonplace, but this one had persistence about it."

David Gallen, in his book *Bill Clinton: As They Know Him,* quotes an anonymous source,

> I seem to recall he was a whirling dervish on the bar circuit during the years he wasn't governor (1980-82). I remember bumping into him in various spots—Bennigans, Busters. That big red nose of his was unmistakable during the Christmas season. He was always with women, with an entourage, and you never knew whether this was his "action" or just staff members but he was always with a pack. His wife was never there. . . . I remember one occasion at Busters. He was working this woman like there was no tomorrow and it was pretty late. . . . His entourage would be around him like Jilly Rizzo around Sinatra, I guess to make it look like he was with a group, but very clearly he was beaming in on one attractive woman. He had good taste. The time we're talking about he closed the deal and left with her right before we did.

It was at this time that a former Little Rock television reporter and lounge singer named Gennifer Flowers would later claim her twelve-year affair with Bill Clinton began. A friend of Bill Clinton described his womanizing at this time as "horrific." At the heart of the couple's marital problems was Clinton's defeat. This marriage was based, at its very core, on the political career of Bill Clinton. For Bill and Hillary, all else was secondary. Even the existence of one-year-old Chelsea did little to quell the dissonance in the relationship. It is telling that when Clinton's political career was shattered, the relationship with his wife was in much the same state.

Although Clinton pouted for a few months after his defeat, there was little doubt he would be running again

in 1982. What else would he do? Clinton went to work at
the Little Rock Law Firm of Wright Lindsey & Jennings,
one of Little Rock's biggest firms. His close friend, Bruce
Lindsey, who would later become Clinton's "fix-it" man
at the White House, provided Clinton with the opportunity. He practiced very little law, as he campaigned full-
time for a year and a half.

"Bill Clinton started campaigning the day after he
lost, after he stopped crying and got his feet back on the
ground," Little Rock businessman Sheffield Nelson recalls. "He realized that the Hillary Rodham thing had to
change, it had to become Hillary Clinton. He realized he
had to drop the arrogance and cut his hair, surround
himself with new people and he had to go tell the people
he was sorry, which he did very effectively."

A short time after his defeat, a determined Clinton
emerged from seclusion with a clear mission. Rex Nelson
wrote, "Bill Clinton and Hillary Rodham would have to
adapt to a new American political ethos that did not
pander to long-haired liberal kids who thought themselves smarter than everybody else. They would have to
adjust or perish."

More importantly, they would have to adjust to an
Arkansas at which they had turned up their noses. At this
point in time, Hillary demonstrated just how committed
she was to her husband's career. Bill's womanizing and
her failing marriage were not enough to deter her from
the power that she sought. She also realized that she was
a problem. Gail Sheehy wrote, "Some say Hillary took
the political defeat harder than her husband
did. . . . Hillary was determined to do whatever it took to
put her husband back in power. So, without a word from
Bill, she shed her name for his. She also dyed her hair,
traded her thick glasses for contacts, and feigned an
interest in fashion."

Dick Hegert, campaign manager of Clinton's 1980
race, told David Gallen that he had pleaded with Hillary.

> I felt very, very strongly that Hillary should change
> her name. I could not get her to do it. I spoke
> before a democratic women's group and at the
> conclusion, before I let them ask me any questions,
> I said, "Let me ask you a question. How important
> do you think it is that Hillary be Hillary Clinton
> rather than Hillary Rodham?" . . . There was mass
> eruption. . . . I left there with the firm opinion that
> the issue was enough to cause us to lose on the
> average of a thousand votes per county. I talked to
> Hillary about it but it's a personal thing. I could
> only press it to a point. We made the point as well
> as we could and very shortly after the election, she
> changed her name.

Although Hillary had said in 1979 that retaining her
maiden name made her feel like a "real person," she
decided to become Mrs. Bill Clinton for the 1982 election. Her husband's political career was far more important than any ideals or values that she had staked out for
herself. A person close to the Clintons at the time remembers Hillary as being upset over having to take Bill's
name, "but Hillary knew that on a political level she had
no choice."

A friend remembers that Hillary really felt like she
was caving in to the public's criticisms, which was something she had never planned on doing. "Hillary had to
concede, everybody knew that it would be politically
advantageous." Donnie Radcliffe wrote of a defeated
Hillary, "Indeed, her self-transformation served as the
ultimate proof of her consistently unemotional and analytical approach to politics; she was able to treat herself
as she would any political asset."

Hillary took a leave of absence from the Rose Law
Firm to campaign full-time with her husband in early
1982. She could usually be found at political events gaz-
ing raptly at her husband with two-year-old Chelsea in
her arms. The *Arkansas Gazette* wrote, "The name change
indicates that she's working at softening her image a bit.

And succeeding, apparently. She has become a good handshaking campaigner in the traditional Arkansas style." Hillary would do her best to avoid controversy and play the role of adoring wife. She meekly stated, "I'm not afraid to speak, but I get very nervous when I'm speaking on behalf of my husband. I fear that something I say might be misconstrued."

In private, her relationship with Bill was at an all-time low. A person close to the Clintons at this time remembers that while Hillary was committed to the campaign, she was privately enraged about the concessions that she had made to Bill. Changing her name, her appearance, and her demeanor, along with becoming a mother, were things that Hillary had resisted. She was also forced to take time out of her career at Rose. Bill's womanizing in 1982 "was particularly bad," and worse, it was now becoming increasingly public. Hillary saw it as a threat to their careers, and she realized the sacrifices she had made were not being reciprocated. She could handle being Mrs. Bill Clinton as long as that meant he was the governor and she was the First Lady.

According to this same person, the situation had deteriorated to one where "Hillary took him by the ear and told him 'you can whore around, but not in public. These are the rules.' " They both sought the power of elected office and the two obviously realized they needed each other to obtain it. On a personal or private level, the two offered each other little support or comfort. They searched elsewhere for that. Many in Arkansas have always considered the marriage a political arrangement or partnership. The Clintons are clearly conscious of this perception.

With a beaming Hillary now at his side, Bill Clinton was forced into an image makeover of his own. In order to project a more "down-home Baptist" public image, Clinton figured he should start going to church. It was in 1981 that Clinton joined Little Rock's influential Immanuel Baptist Church and became a regular churchgoer. Up to that point in time, Clinton described himself as "an uneven churchgoer for a long time." He even joined the choir. Gov. Frank White received strong support from fundamentalist Christians and other church groups. Clinton's newfound interest in religion was nothing more than politics.

White never really had a chance as governor. As Winthrop Rockefeller had learned in the 1960s, the Democratic state legislature made it very difficult for a Republican governor to get anything accomplished. During White's term, the 135-member Arkansas General Assembly had only 7 Republican members. His lack of experience in public office hurt him as well. He had campaigned with the pledge that he would run the state government like a business. It didn't take him long to realize that the Arkansas political system was incapable of conforming to sound business principles. As Clinton had learned, the government was still essentially controlled by an all-powerful Democratic party whose decisions were based largely on cronyism and political patronage. The press was merciless in their attacks on White, and they were still in love with Clinton, whom they had strongly supported in the 1980 race.

Clinton had learned his lesson well. He turned to old-time machine characters. John Robert Starr wrote, "His headquarters had been manned by an effective mix of old political hands like former state auditor Jimmie (Red) Jones and Highway Commissioners George Kell and Maurice Smith, both of whom had extensive experience in political campaigns, Kell mostly with Dale Bumpers and Smith with Orval Faubus." The hiring of former Faubus aides demonstrated just how far he was willing to go in order to placate the Democrats, especially those who controlled the rural counties.

Clinton's top aide in this race, and in his subsequent terms as governor, was Betsey Wright. The two had met in Texas while working on the ill-fated McGovern campaign. Interestingly, she arrived in Little Rock a scant ten days after Clinton's 1980 defeat to get things in order for the 1982 race. Wright explains, "He called me about a week after the election in which he was defeated and asked if I would come see if there was anything that could be salvaged of his political career in case he ever had an opportunity to run again for something so I went back and helped close down the governor's office." Wright claimed, "We weren't sure he was going to run two years later. We didn't really know whether it was possible or not until we did a benchmark poll in the fall of 1981, so for almost a year, running in 1982 wasn't exactly what we were working on." She actually had office space with Clinton at Wright, Lindsey and Jennings for most of 1981.

With Wright engineering the negative campaign, the 1982 race was fought in the gutter. Clinton and "Queen Betsey," as Wright would come to be known, would prove to be more than up to the task. This race, by all accounts, was the dirtiest in the state's history.

Hillary, too, was very much involved in the campaign's decision making. Political writer Rex Nelson wrote, "Throughout the 1982 campaign Hillary maintained a higher profile than she had two years earlier. Yet still, much of her work was behind the scenes, offering advice and helping Wright plan strategy." The campaign was her full-time job. The Rose firm was supportive of Hillary's leave of absence. They had a vested interest in seeing her husband retain the governorship. Obviously, her value to the firm was based in large part on her husband's political standing.

In the end, Clinton defeated White with 54.7 percent of the vote. In 1993, Frank White explained his loss by pointing out that Clinton had captured 93 percent of the black vote. "The first time around (1980) Clinton didn't think he had to pay for those votes. He was too cocky. He learned his lesson, from that first defeat on he had the preachers in his pocket."

In Arkansas this practice is known as "hauling" the black vote. Diane Blair explained in 1986, "Candidates expecting large turnouts in many black communities are still expected to foot the bill for 'knockers and haulers' (those who knock on doors and drive carloads of voters to the polls) and for other 'election day' expenses. This is a contemporary version of the traditional 'walking around money' and at least through 1986 is still considered essential." The practice persists to this day.

According to a high-ranking state official, the price tag for securing the black vote is somewhere between $250,000 and $300,000. "The system is controlled by the preachers. Everything from a new set of choir robes to chickens for parishioners, anything goes, as long as they get out the vote." The black vote in Arkansas elections amounts to close to 20 percent of the overall vote.

Mrs. Bill Clinton, who had played the game during this campaign, was ready to reap the rewards for her efforts. She would exploit her position in many ways, including her insistence on chairing the state's Education Standards Committee, her career at the Rose Law Firm, and in other out-of-state activities. Knowing what she did about Bill Clinton's personal life, Hillary's power was derived not simply from her standing as First Lady. Her power was based on the control that she had over Bill Clinton, a man she was capable of destroying with one press conference.

Six

The Clinton Decade

In January of 1983, Hillary triumphantly moved her meager belongings, mostly books, back into the governor's mansion. Hillary had trouble hiding her glee on that glorious day. In her mind, this was the only acceptable Arkansas residence. Mr. and Mrs. Bill Clinton would have a stranglehold on Arkansas for the next ten years.

On 11 January, "Happy Days Are Here Again" was played as Bill and Hillary arrived at the inaugural ball in the ballroom of Little Rock's new Excelsior Hotel, a place that would be made famous twelve years later by Paula Corbin Jones. The nine-hundred-person affair was described by Clinton as a "nice little intimate party for a few friends." Hillary had indeed learned from her past mistakes. This night she wore a simple, elegant gown which stood in marked contrast to the embarrassing outfit she had worn to the inaugural ball in 1978. These were high times for the Clintons. They had worked their way back and were determined to stay.

The day's events were disrupted a bit for Hillary when her father, Hugh, had to be taken to the hospital. Suffering from severe chest pains, he had to leave the ceremonies. The seventy-one-year-old Hugh did not have a heart attack, but his condition was serious, necessitating a triple coronary bypass later that week.

Upon winning back the governorship, Clinton made education his number one priority, even though he had paid little attention to the issue in his first term. No one objected. Arkansas was ranked either dead last or near the bottom in all statistical categories. Only halting progress had been made since 1922, when a federal government report stated,

> For thousands upon thousands of children, Arkansas is providing absolutely no chance. To these children, to be born in Arkansas is a misfortune and an injustice from which they will never recover and upon which they will look back with bitterness when plunged, in adult life, into competition with children born in other states which are today providing more liberally for their children.

In a sense, Clinton didn't really have a choice in making education a priority. The state supreme court had recently declared the state's system of financing education unconstitutional, citing a great disparity in funding between rich and poor school districts. In his inaugural address Clinton stated,

> Over the long run, education is the key to our economic revival and our perennial quest for prosperity. We must dedicate more of our limited resources to paying our teachers better; expanding educational opportunities in poor and small school districts; improving and diversifying vocational and high technology programs; and, perhaps most important, strengthening basic education.

On 22 April Bill Clinton announced the creation of a fifteen-member task force called the Education Standards Committee, and named his wife as chairman. The group was charged with the formidable task of overhauling Arkansas' education system. Clearly, Hillary had hand-picked this position for herself. Clinton would later claim that the two had been offhandedly discussing the subject of the chairmanship when Hillary said, "I think I'd like to be it. Maybe I'll do it." It is unlikely that the decision was arrived at so casually. Meredith Oakley of the *Arkan-*

sas-Democrat Gazette remembers that "they needed to build Hillary's popularity which was much lower than his and so they created that position for her. And, of course, she shone, as she was destined to do in that position. That was a prefabricated issue."

It was a perfect opportunity for Hillary to reintroduce herself to the public. Although she combed her hair and dressed a little better, she still had an image problem. It was time to present a softer personality. The goal of improving education had no critics, and the endeavor was appropriate for a First Lady. Although Hillary claimed that she would suffer "financial disadvantages," she took a leave of absence from the Rose Law Firm to chair the panel.

She had no experience or expertise in education. Undaunted, she acknowledged the obvious: "I've gone to school a large part of my life, and I've been involved in classroom activities and visiting with teachers as a volunteer. But I don't come to this job with a great deal of expertise." Kai Erickson, an official of the Arkansas Education Association, recalled to *Mother Jones,* "It appeared she pretty much had in mind what she planned to do. She was a little brusque. I thought the issues and challenges would cause one who was not an expert to be more tentative than she was."

The campaign for education reform is remembered more for the process than the result. Over the next four months, Hillary presided over hearings in all seventy-five counties. The hearings were attended by everyone involved in education, from superintendents to students. The gatherings seemed to accomplish little in the way of substance. Their purpose seemed to be to introduce the new Hillary to rural Arkansans and to create the political momentum for passage by the legislature of the reforms the committee came up with.

Connie Bruck wrote in *The New Yorker* in May 1994, "While this process triumphantly established Hillary Clinton's bonafides with a considerable segment of the population of Arkansas, that may have been its chief accomplishment. It was designed to look like an exhaustive fact-finding process (hence the seventy-five hearings), which would culminate in the deliberations of the committee and conclude with its recommendations." According to Kai Erickson, "Those meetings were set up by the governor's office. They were political—basically, getting people to agree there was a problem, so that the solutions already devised would be accepted. It was to look like fact-finding. Hillary probably picked up a few things here and there, but not much."

The reform effort had the look and feel of a political campaign. The Clintons put on an all-out assault. Led by campaign veteran Betsey Wright, they used professional pollsters and private public relations firms. Slick materials were sent out in an orchestrated mail campaign, promoting not only education reform, but the Clintons themselves, who were portrayed as smart, caring, and progressive.

Hillary's speeches were given in an earnest, down-home manner. They frequently contained lines like:

> Our state has tremendous opportunity because we are poised on the brink of a real growth period. We have a tradition of people who know how to work, who are willing to make sacrifices, who sometimes can get more done with less than other folks. They are people who, if given a chance to acquire a good education, will really respond. There is a real readiness out there to do something about education. People who never gave it a thought five years ago, who don't even have children in school, are really understanding the link between a good education and future quality of life. They want something done. . . . There is a constituency out there that is growing for a good education system for our children. I like being part of something that I believe can make a significant difference in people's lives.

Hillary released her committee's findings in July of 1983 to a special legislative committee of the state House of Representatives, and to a similar Senate committee a month later. Hillary impressed the House committee by patiently and efficiently answering the legislators' questions for more than ninety minutes. Rep. Lloyd George (D-Russselville) pronounced, "I think we elected the wrong Clinton." Ten years later, Hillary would testify on Capitol Hill on the findings of her health care task force. House Ways and Means Committee Chairman Dan Rostenkowski would echo George, "In the very near future, I think the president will be known as your husband. People will say, 'Who's that fellow?' "

While welcomed by the lawmakers, the recommendations were far from revolutionary. They included mandatory kindergarten, longer school days and longer school years, reduction of the student-teacher ratio, increases in teacher salaries, more required courses, and the establishment of the Minimum Performance Tests (MPT) to be given to students completing the third, sixth, and eighth grades. Nina Martin wrote years later in the left-wing *Mother Jones* that "only in a state like Arkansas would such a minor package—improved curriculum, student testing, higher salaries—be labeled 'reform.' "

The reform proposals were not very original, either. They were similar to plans that were already implemented in nearby states. Mississippi Gov. William Winter had already won praise for an education program put into place before Clinton resumed office in 1983. So did Gov. Lamar Alexander of Tennessee, who went on to serve as education secretary in the Bush administration. Meredith Oakley wrote in 1991, "As far as innovation goes, Clinton's accomplishments in the mid-1980s pale beside those of then-Gov. Lamar Alexander, whose 12-point education reform package set a standard Clinton openly envied but never was able to duplicate."

Many of the proposals were not new for Arkansas, either. In fact, a number were drawn straight from previous in-state resources. The first was the so-called Alexander Report, which had been commissioned by the state legislature in 1978. The second was a proposed law called the Quality Education Act, which had been drafted by the Arkansas Education Association in 1979.

Connie Bruck wrote,

> Experts agree that a number of the committee's recommendations were substantially similar to an initiative that had been proposed by the Arkansas Education Association in 1979. Not only did the blueprint already exist but the committee—in calling for smaller class sizes, more required courses in every high school, and the establishment of state-administered Minimum Performance Tests to be given in the third, sixth, and eighth grades—was far from the vanguard.

At about the same time that Hillary was beginning her work on educational standards, a national report, "Nation at Risk," was released. The report painted a bleak picture for the future of American education and warned of a "rising tide of mediocrity." Hillary borrowed heavily from its themes and called the report a "blueprint for how we get ourselves out of the serious state of deterioration we're currently in."

The Clintons' campaign went into overdrive once Hillary had presented her findings to the various legislative committees. They raised $130,000 in contributions to fuel the campaign. Hillary traveled throughout the state during the summer of 1983 promoting the theme "a time for change." Bill, meanwhile, was selling the reforms to legislators. The reform package would have been a legislative "slam dunk" except for one thing. In order to pay for the new standards, a tax increase would be necessary. Roy Reed, a former reporter for the *Arkansas Gazette*, remembers that Clinton "felt for the hidden seed of pride in the hillbilly breast. Every speech contained a sure-fire goad: Even Mississippi is ahead of us now."

Clinton proposed raising the state sales tax one cent. John Robert Starr wrote, "By the time Clinton called the legislature into special session on October 4, the people were convinced that raising the sales tax one cent on the dollar was a small price to pay for an educational system that would allow Arkansas public school graduates to compete both nationally and internationally." According to Betsey Wright, "No legislature has ever come close to being begged to raise taxes as that one was when it finally convened." Clinton also tried to obtain a 1 percent increase in the corporate income tax and an increase in the severance tax. He was unable to pass this part of the financing, however, and the entire burden of the tax increase was placed on the people with the regressive 1 percent sales tax.

Charles Allen asserted in his sympathetic Clinton biography, "If Bill Clinton's reforms were going to be realized, they would have to be paid for with a sales tax. The corporate interests of Arkansas had declined to pay for school reform. For all his talk of risking his career for the program, Bill Clinton was not ready to risk it in a major fight with the business community. This was a watershed. Bill Clinton's 'idealism' had vanished, to be replaced with an expedient pragmatism."

Bill Clinton called a special legislative session in October to consider the reforms. He unveiled a surprise when he went on statewide television the day before the legislative session opened: teachers would be subjected to a competency test. The tests, deeply resented by teachers, had not been a part of the standards that Hillary had presented to the legislature. The original draft of the Standards Committee recommendations did not include teacher testing. Teacher competency was addressed in broad terms, such as a recommendation that teachers be certified and a finding that they would benefit from additional educational experience. Hillary did make a vague reference to "accountability" in testimony before the legislature: "The problem of teacher accountability begins in higher education, and we think teacher education is inadequate in many respects. The governor is quite probably looking at teacher accountability in the context of his overall recommendations." But, that was it. When Hillary introduced the new standards at a 7 September news conference, she had made no mention of the teacher tests.

Many believed that the testing was nothing more than a political move on the part of the Clintons. As the medical profession would discover in 1993, politicians sometimes need to create a villain. In order to justify the tax and spending increase, Clinton had to somehow demonstrate that someone would be accountable for the way the funds would be spent.

The Arkansas Education Association (AEA), a union affiliated with the National Education Association, has traditionally backed liberals for public office. AEA supported the efforts of Hillary's reform committee and considered itself an ally of the Clinton administration. The proposal for teacher tests was considered a betrayal and created a rift with the administration. An AEA official named Sid Johnson told *Mother Jones* in 1993, "She snookered us good. I was feeling the same as I suppose doctors do now."

Teachers felt that they were being unfairly scapegoated for the abysmal state of education in Arkansas. Many viewed the tests as not only a political ploy but an affront to their profession. Worse, the idea seemed to have racist overtones. Kai Erickson said, "There was a great schism. The idea of a teacher test was understood to have appeal to those white parents who felt that black teachers were not competent. The black teachers, though, felt that it was racist." Clinton supporter Max Brantley, then editor of the *Arkansas Gazette*, told Connie Bruck in 1994, "The teacher test was a cynical ploy. It was a meaningless test. It did little to improve the quality of teaching. It was clearly done to get the tax increase." When asked years later by Bruck about the racist nature of the campaign, an Arkansas liberal like Hillary's close friend Henry Woods, now a federal judge, could only respond, "Well, but they couldn't have passed the legislation without it."

The special education legislative session lasted thirty-eight days and the tax increase was ultimately approved by both the House and Senate in November 1983. The new standards, including teacher testing, became law. "I think we have a really good set of standards—a blueprint that Arkansas can follow over the next few years," Hillary stated. "This is a move toward competency-based education and the requirement of more accountability and responsibility from students, teachers, the school systems and parents." The standards were officially adopted in February 1984 with an implementation date of July 1987.

By the mid-nineties, after the reforms had been fully implemented for several years, no appreciable improvement in Arkansas education had taken place. Measured in a variety of ways, Arkansas continues to trail almost every other state. In 1995, Ed Crow, an official of the Arkansas Higher Education Department, explained, "There has always been a relationship between family income and test performance. It's not an excuse for lower scores, but it is one explanation. To change that, we have got to change the economy of the state."

When he ran for president, Clinton campaigned on the fact that he had done just that. Not all Arkansans agreed. The *Arkansas Democrat-Gazette* editorialized in 1992, "Statistics abound that give the lie to Bill Clinton's myth about his saving Arkansas from 150 years of squalor: Median family income in this state stalled at 49th in the union after a decade of Clintonism. Per capita income in Arkansas went from 75.4 percent of the national average in 1980 to 76.8 percent in 1990, a gain of only 1.4 percent in ten years. This is a success story?"

Today, the impact of the education reforms is discounted by both Clinton friend and foe. Little Rock businessman Blant Hurt wrote in a 1993 *Wall Street Jour-*

nal column, "Did Mrs. Clinton's efforts as Arkansas's education czar deliver results? The answer is no, at least if we count only favorable ones."

Long-time Little Rock radio talk-show host Bill Powell opined, "When he [Clinton] took office we were forty-ninth, forty-eighth, and forty-seventh in all statistical indicators. We're still forty-ninth, forty-eighth, and forty seventh. The only difference is it's costing us five times more than it did when he took office."

Gloria Cabe, a former Clinton aide, says, "It was really just bringing Arkansas in line with the rest of the country. The single greatest outcome of Hillary's work was that Arkansas began to value education more. It was that, more than anything specific, demonstrable improvement."

To the extent that the education reforms are defended, it is not on the basis that they made a difference, but that they effected a change in attitude. Ernie Dumas, formerly of the *Arkansas Gazette*, claims that the Clintons "changed attitudes about education in Arkansas." Mahlon Martin, former Clinton staff member, asserts that "after the 1983 initiative and even up through the time he left, there was just a whole different mind set around education. People were still critical of some of the things that went on in the system but they really embraced education as important. The changing of the mind set was as important as anything he did." According to former Clinton aide Don Ernst, "Hillary used this as an opportunity to engage the people of Arkansas for the first time in a real conversation about education. To me, that was the most significant accomplishment."

Even some sympathetic to the reforms were not sold on Clinton's sincerity. John Robert Starr said, "I think he cares about the reading level of school kids as long as it doesn't interfere with his personal agenda. If he were to see a poll tomorrow saying that the people wanted the public education abandoned, that 99 percent of the people wanted to abandon public education, he would run there. He's what (former Arkansas Supreme Court Justice) Jim

Johnson calls the kind of leader that finds out which way
the crowd's going and then runs around and gets in front
and says, 'follow me.' "

Bill Clinton was reelected governor in 1984, easily
defeating Republican Woody Freeman after Frank White
decided to sit out the race. Clinton was reelected in 1986
in another bloody battle with White. He would not face
the voters again for four years, due to a change in the law
extending the term from two to four years.

In 1990, he defeated Republican Sheffield Nelson
for an unprecedented fifth term as governor. In unequivo-
cal language, with none of the usual escape clauses,
Clinton told the people that he would not run for president if they reelected him in 1990. During a debate with
Sheffield Nelson on 15 October 1990, Bill Clinton was
asked by newsman Craig Cannon, "Will you guarantee all
of us that if re-elected there is absolutely, positively no
way that you'll run for any other political office and that
you'll serve your term out in full?" Clinton replied, "You
bet. I told you when I announced for governor I intended to run and that's what I'm going to do. I'm gonna
serve four years. I made that decision when I decided to
run. I'm being considered as a candidate for governor.
That's the job I want. That's the job I'll do for the next
four years."

Bill Clinton would announce his candidacy for the
presidency less than a year later on 3 October 1991.
There is no doubt that he knew he would be running for
president when he answered Craig Cannon's question.
The *Arkansas Democrat* headlined the story of Clinton's
scheduled announcement to run for president this way:
"Clinton will officially break his promise to Arkansans
today."

Clinton had come very close to running for president
in 1988. When Arkansas Sen. Dale Bumpers announced
that he would not run, many people thought that Clinton
would enter the race. But, Gary Hart had been forced
out of the race because of an extramarital affair with

Donna Rice, and this had a tremendous impact on his decision not to run.

Clinton's womanizing had become a serious political problem by 1988. The Clintons' relationship was at a very low point, even by their standards. Clinton was talking to political friends who had dealt with divorce in their careers. Betsey Wright explained to David Maraniss that she confronted Clinton as he was contemplating entering the 1988 race. According to Wright, she and Clinton sat down in her living room one evening,

> then she started listing the names of women he had allegedly had affairs with and the places where they were said to have occurred. She went over the list twice with Clinton, according to her later account, the second time trying to determine whether any of the women might tell their stories to the press. At the end of the process, she suggested that he should not get into the race. He owed it to Hillary and Chelsea not to.

Clinton, with friends from around the country present, announced he would not run for president in 1988. Hillary had tears in her eyes. He claimed that he was sitting the race out because of his daughter, who was only seven years old. A Republican state legislator who was present at the announcement can remember a Democratic colleague leaning over and saying to him, "He'd throw Chelsea in that dumpster over there if it meant he could be president."

Of course, a divorce was not an option for Hillary. She told Betsey Wright that she was unwilling to give up all that she had invested in their partnership. Through the 1980s Hillary, Betsey Wright, and Press Secretary Joan Roberts were Clinton's closest advisors. Wright and Roberts skillfully managed the governor's office, the legislature, and the press. Hillary, close by, kept an eye on her investment. Although her work on education helped her standing with the Arkansas public, she was still not the complete picture of a traditional First Lady. Most significantly, she pursued a full-time career at the Rose firm. Perhaps as a rationalization for staying in her failing marriage with Bill and her acceptance of his philandering, Hillary exploited her position as the wife of the governor with vigor, especially when it came to financial opportunities.

Sympathetic reporters have not failed to point out that Hillary was named one of the country's top one hundred lawyers by the *National Law Journal* in 1988 and 1991. In actuality, she was named one of the top one hundred "most influential" lawyers in the country, a designation that had more to do with who her husband was. Hillary did very little lawyering, and when she did, it often pertained to her own financial and political interests. According to *The American Lawyer*, Hillary tried only five cases in her career at Rose. Said one former Rose lawyer in 1992, "My view is, she does not contribute much as a lawyer. But she is Bill Clinton's wife, and they feel good about that." Hillary spent the Decade of Greed, as her liberal brethren labeled the eighties, pursuing a host of questionable business activities that ran the gamut from the unethical to the fraudulent.

As L. J. Davis wrote in *The New Republic* in 1994,

> With Rodham Clinton aboard at Rose, the firm's long established connections to the governor's office were firmer still. Rose, the gold standard of Arkansas law firms, had long enjoyed unusual access to the state's corridors of power . . . and during the Clinton years, the Rose Law Firm sometimes behaved as though it were an agency of the state rather than a legal partnership with offices in a converted YMCA.

C. Joseph Giroir was the first and only chairman of the Rose firm. Under his leadership, the firm grew from seventeen lawyers to fifty-three between 1975 and 1988. He was ousted in 1988 after he was sued by two major banks, which also happened to be long-time clients of the firm. Giroir was deeply involved with the banking interests across the state, and the conflicts of interest he created became too much for the firm. It is also believed that disagreements over the firm's compensation system caused a coup of sorts from the firm's other lawyers. The takeover was engineered by the firm's most influential lawyers: Hillary, Webster Hubbell, and Vincent Foster.

Audrey Duff wrote in *The American Lawyer* in 1992,

> Whatever the reasons for Giroir's departure in 1988, since then Foster, Hubbell, and Clinton have come to wield significant power in the firm. In Clinton's case, it would appear, this is more because of who she is than what she does. While there is no denying her blue-chip legal credentials, her caseload appears light. But in a firm still grappling with the loss of a single leader and dedicated to consensus-based management style, Clinton's forthright personality seems to carry her far. Her pugnaciousness and outspokenness are legendary.

Diane Blair described the relationship between Hillary, Hubbell, and Foster: "They were so great to-gether—like basketball players, where they can pass and don't even have to look." The bond between Hillary and Foster seemed to be the strongest. Connie Bruck quoted a White House source saying, "Vince Foster worshipped her. He would have done anything for her." Hubbell was also close to Bill, who has described Hubbell as his best friend; the two of them would often play golf together.

Hubbell authored Arkansas' government ethics law, passed in 1988. As originally written, the legislation re-quired public officials, including the governor, to file detailed reports of outside business activities. In the Clintons' case, it would have included those of his wife. The bill passed the legislature overwhelmingly only to be hung up in the state senate for reasons unrelated to the disclosure issue. The bill was then redrafted by Hubbell to conveniently exempt the governor and his family from any conflict-of-interest disclosure. The new bill was passed and signed into law by Clinton. Hubbell probably should have been less cynical about ethics. In 1994, he would resign from the Clinton Justice Department and be sentenced to prison for bilking Rose clients, including the federal government, for close to $400,000.

The only Rose partners who were allowed to sit on corporate boards were Hillary and, before his departure, Joe Giroir. This proved to be a lucrative activity for Hillary. She collected $64,000 annually in director's fees from Wal-Mart, TCBY, and the LaFarge Corporation. Her income at Rose had grown steadily in the 1980s from $24,000 in 1978, to $92,000 in 1989, to $109,000 in 1991, to $203,000 in 1992. Wal-Mart and TCBY were both based in Arkansas, while LaFarge was based in Virginia. She amassed stock in Wal-Mart that was valued between $100,000 and $250,000, according to her federal disclosure statement filed in 1993.

These figures present a far different picture of Clinton family finances than that portrayed during the 1992 campaign when Bill boasted about his "lowest-in-the nation" $35,000 governor's salary. The Clintons were embarrassed in August 1993 by a widely publicized article in *The American Spectator*, in which Lisa Schiffren detailed how "all Clinton personal living expenses (including food, shelter, transportation and entertainment), along with security, housekeeping, administration, utilities, etc., were paid out of various state funds" during the years he served as governor. Arkansas taxpayers provided a mansion, Lincoln Town Cars, nannies, cooks, drivers, food, and every other household expense. According to the Arkansas state Auditor, the upkeep of the Clintons cost $750,000 annually.

Included in this amount was a $19,000 "public relations" fund, from which Bill sent flowers or fruit baskets to constituents, as well as a $3,500 fund for "personal entertainment." The First Family received an unrestricted $51,000 food allotment. Lisa Schiffren wrote that the fund was "intended for both state functions and private meals, as well as incidental mansion expenses and anything else the governor might wish to spend it on. Unlike most expense funds, but like income, that stipend was not subject to oversight by the state legislature." Because it was discretionary, it probably should have been reported as income on their tax returns. Schiffren contacted former IRS Commissioner Donald Alexander, who opined that the Clintons' failure to report the $51,000 "probably constitutes a failure to report income."

Hillary had no problem finding deductions for her tax returns, meticulously listing small amounts for clothing and toys donated to the Salvation Army and Goodwill. Her deductions totaled between $1,000 and $2,300 annually for these items. She went so far as to list Bill's underwear as a $1 deduction. Campaign T-shirts were deducted at $3, and used running shoes were worth $10 in Hillary's mind.

Other deductions were even more curious. In 1994, Ken Boehm of the National Legal and Policy Center, a Washington-based ethics watchdog, reviewed Hillary's deductions during her tenure as part-time chairman of Legal Services Corporation from 1978 to 1982. In 1979 Hillary reported $8,823 in gross income from LSC. Against this she found deductions of $555 for automobile expenses, $1,116 for a desk, $120 for shelving, $750 for a sofa and $57 for books. Why did Hillary need to buy a desk and sofa for her work with Legal Services? She was living in the governor's mansion and working at the Rose Law Firm. The LSC office in Washington, used by directors when they are in town, is furnished, too. When queried about such deductions in 1994, a former LSC director claimed the deductions were "way out of line and unheard of." Mike Wallace, a former LSC board chairman, found the deductions equally inappropriate: "Purchases of equipment? That's a new one on me."

Between 1978 and 1981, Hillary made three trades in the stock of DeBeers, the South African diamond company, resulting in profits of $1,591. According to Randall Robinson, director of the anti-apartheid group Trans-Africa, "While there may have been those who invested in American companies who were unaware of their involvement in South Africa, to purchase stock in DeBeers is to virtually support apartheid directly." Hillary has claimed that she knew nothing of the trades and that her money had been in a discretionary account. When various instances of questionable financial dealings have come to light, she has taken the same or a similar tact.

In 1983 Hillary, Hubbell, and Foster created something called Mid-Life Investors. Each contributed $15,000 and named each other as beneficiaries, not their spouses. It was Hillary who contacted Roy Drew at E.F. Hutton in Little Rock to set up the account. According to Drew, Hillary was the one who kept track of the account. By his recollections, Hillary would call "three or four times a week," and would seek explanations for movements as minuscule as an eighth of a point. "She was very unsophisticated but highly interested," Drew recalls. "She was clearly someone who wanted to make a buck."

In 1984 Hillary invested $2,014 with a group led by David Watkins that was applying for a license to run a local cellular phone franchise. Investor Larry Wallace explained that Hillary was recruited to the group for her "marquee value." The group got the franchise and subsequently sold it to McCaw Cellular Communications. Hillary received a check for $45,998 when the deal was done. Watkins ended up in the White House with Hillary, only to be sent home in disgrace after being caught using a government helicopter for a 1994 golfing trip to Maryland.

A 1989 deal involving nursing homes in Iowa sheds light on the way the Rose Law Firm operated with Hillary, Hubbell, and Foster in charge. Rose represented Beverly Enterprises, the country's largest operator of nursing homes, in the sale of forty-five nursing homes in Iowa. Beverly was controlled by the powerful Stephens family of Little Rock, Rose's top client. The parties in the deal took advantage of tax breaks available to charities. By using a shell charity called Mercy Health Initiatives, which had no office or employees, the sale was financed through the issuance of $85 million in tax-exempt bonds by the Iowa state finance authority. In one day, Rose's client netted $10 million. Rose's fee was estimated at $500,000. The losers in this transaction were the elderly residents of the homes whose fees were raised 14 percent to cover the excessive costs of the purchase.

Iowa tax authorities would later successfully challenge Mercy Health's tax-exempt status in 1991. Iowa Judge Gene Needles concluded that Mercy Health "served no legitimate purpose and was used primarily to obtain tax-exempt financing, shield the parties using the facilities from liability and obligations as owners and evade the payment of property taxes." He also called the participants in the scam "unconscionable profiteers."

During her health care campaign in 1993, Hillary would condemn "price gouging" and "unconscionable profiteering" in the health industry. As Richard Brookhiser put it in *National Review*,

> Rose Law could have collected as much as a half a million dollars for shuffling the papers, to be divided in bonuses among its partners, including Hillary Rodham. Meanwhile, the nursing homes, in order to pay off their debt, were forced to raise fees. The nursing home deal, all perfectly legal, offered a foretaste of the Clinton health plan: everyone was screwed, except the large medical corporations and the lawyers.

The Rose firm tried to duplicate the very same deal in Arkansas in 1989, this time using Governor Clinton's Arkansas Development Finance Authority (ADFA) to issue the tax-exempt bonds. The deal never went through. Attorney General Steve Clark, whose approval was required for the deal, disclosed that he had been offered a one-hundred-thousand-dollar campaign contribution, which he called a "bribe," to support the bond proposal. In December of 1989 Clinton was forced to withdraw support for the ADFA loan. Alexander Cockburn wrote in *The Nation* in 1994, "Of course, back in '89 when Clinton was using his home-spun rhetoric to present himself as the state's guardian against corporate exploitation, he never let on that Rose Law was the forward guard for those exploiters. Since then, he and Hillary and anyone else who's asked from the firm have stonewalled questions about the case."

According to a Rose lawyer, "All partners were aware of all deals, and shared in profits." Roy Drew, the Little Rock stockbroker who helped set up Mid-Life investors, is familiar with the machinations of the nursing home deal. He told Cockburn in 1994, "If Hillary Clinton made a buck—if she made even one dollar on those nursing home deals—she shouldn't be on the stump talking about unconscionable profits." Hillary did indeed take her partner's share on the Iowa deal.

One month later, Steve Clark, who had blown the whistle on the nursing home deal, was the target of an investigation by the Arkansas State Police into the misuse of his state expense account. He was convicted in a well-publicized trial and fined ten thousand dollars. Clark's political career was over and he left the state.

The inherent conflict of interest between Hillary's legal work and the political career of her husband is demonstrated even more clearly in the case of Dan Lasater. A long-time friend of Bill's and a campaign contributor, Lasater was a bond trader who was accused of defrauding First American of Oak Brook, Illinois. The S&L collapsed and left taxpayers with some $88 million in bad debts. The Federal Savings and Loan Insurance Corporation (FSLIC) sued Lasater for fraud and hired the Rose Law Firm as outside counsel. Hillary and Vince Foster were assigned to the case. Hillary arranged an out-of-court settlement, whereby Lasater had to pay only $200,000 to get the $3.3 million lawsuit dismissed.

Hillary failed to disclose her relationship with Lasater to her client, the federal government, when she accepted the case. This was more than a minor conflict of interest. Lasater was not only a contributor to her husband's campaigns, but a family friend. Lasater employed Clinton's brother, Roger, and claimed he once gave him $8,000 to pay off drug debts.

Lasater was more than the average S&L crook. In a 1994 *New Republic* piece, L.J. Davis described Lasater as

> a man no governor in his right mind would let in the front door. If Dan Lasater was not the largest cocaine user in the state of Arkansas, he was certainly the most conspicuous one. . . . He served ashtrays full of cocaine at parties in his mansion, stocked cocaine on his corporate jet (a plane used by the Clintons on more than one occasion) and later told the FBI that he had distributed cocaine on more than 180 occasions.

In 1985 Governor Clinton awarded Lasater & Co. a $30.2 million bond issue to upgrade the state police's communication system, which would ultimately earn Lasater $750,000 in underwriting fees. At the time Clinton was lobbying the state legislature on Lasater's behalf, the police were investigating his drug activities. In 1986 Lasater was arrested and sentenced to two and a half years in prison. It was while Lasater was in jail that Hillary brokered the settlement in the Illinois S&L case. Lasater was pardoned by Governor Clinton in 1991.

As strange and reckless as these relationships might seem, the Clintons have repeatedly denied any wrongdoing and have offered a variety of explanations. Similarly, they have simply tried to explain away their involvement in Whitewater, the one deal to which the national media has paid attention.

Jim McDougal and Bill Clinton were old friends, having worked together in Senator Fulbright's office while Bill was at Georgetown. By the late 1970s, McDougal had made a name for himself in real estate. He had turned some quick profits not only for himself, but for others as well, including Senator Fulbright. In June of 1978, McDougal and his wife Susan, along with Bill and Hillary Clinton, formed the Whitewater Development Corporation and purchased two hundred acres of land on Arkansas' White River for development as vacation lots. Bill was the state's attorney general at the time, and would soon become governor. As governor, he appointed McDougal as a liaison to the Economic Development Department.

On 2 July 1978 the Clintons and McDougals signed a $182,611 mortgage loan from Citizens Bank of Flippin (AR). The down payment for the purchase of the land was $20,000, which was secured by a loan from Union National Bank. Jim McDougal and Bill Clinton signed for the loan. One hundred percent of the project was financed on borrowed money. The plan was to resell the White River lots for a quick profit, but the real estate market declined as interest rates soared, leaving the investors with mounting debt.

The Clintons have always claimed that they assumed 50 percent of the risk, that their investment was not protected by McDougal, and that they did not benefit in any way from McDougal. Furthermore, they have maintained that they were "passive investors" and that McDougal made the investment decisions. At an April 1994 White House news conference, Hillary went even further. "The ownership of the corporation was 50-50. The liability on the underlying debt was 100 percent for each one of us." Had McDougal not paid his share, Hillary claimed, "we would not only have been left with 50 percent of the obligation, we would have had 100 percent of the obligation."

On 16 July 1995, under the headline "Documents Show Clintons Got Vast Benefit From Their Partner in Whitewater Deal," the *New York Times* reported on the first independent review of Whitewater. The study was done for the Resolution Trust Corporation by the San

Francisco-based law firm of Pillsbury, Madison and Sutro in April of 1995. The report refutes the assertion that the Clintons paid an equal share of the losses. The report concludes that Whitewater's losses were about $200,000. The Clintons contributed $42,192 to Whitewater, and McDougal and his wife put in the rest—$158,523.

Hillary had to know that she had not paid 50 percent of the venture's losses. RTC investigator L. Jean Lewis says that the Clintons "knew they had real estate ventures that were not cash flowing, but also knew that their mortgages and/or notes were being paid. . . . These business partners were intelligent individuals, the majority of them being lawyers who must have concluded that McDougal was making payments for their benefit."

In an action undercutting her claim as a "passive investor," Hillary took out a loan in 1980 for $30,000 to build a prefab house on Lot 13 at the entrance of the Whitewater development to help spur lot sales. She received the loan from the Bank of Kingston, owned by Jim McDougal. Ultimately, McDougal and Whitewater would make the payments on this loan. According to the 1995 RTC report, Hillary responded to a 1982 past due notice from the bank, "I ask that you speak with Mr. or Mrs. McDougal, who have made all the arrangements for this loan. It has been my understanding that the loan has been paid out of proceeds from sales by the Whitewater Development Corporation."

When the lot and house were sold in 1988, the Clintons received about $1,600 in profit from the sale. The *New York Times* reported in August 1995, "The tangled tale of Lot 13 did not surface again until 1992, when Mr. McDougal expressed irritation that he had put $100,000 more than the Clintons in Whitewater, including payments to the bank for Lot 13, and that Mrs. Clinton had then sold the lot for a profit to her and her husband."

Clearly, the Clintons benefited by their relationship with McDougal. Did McDougal receive anything in return?

Jim McDougal bought a small bank in Augusta, Arkansas, in 1982. He changed the name of the bank to Madison Guaranty and moved it to the fashionable Quapaw section of Little Rock. The bank's assets mushroomed from $6 million to $123 million in four years. McDougal offered high interest rates to depositors, and eventually persuaded Little Rock's elite to take part in various real estate deals. But, McDougal would eventually find himself overextended in a myriad of bad deals and real estate investments. "If you had to pick the typical failed S&L, Madison would fit the profile," says S&L expert Bert Ely. "It had every symptom: low capital, rapid growth, non-traditional investments, excessive compensation for its officers, etc."

At about the same time, McDougal retained the Rose firm and Hillary at the request of Bill Clinton. The Clintons deny Bill asked McDougal to hire Hillary, but Rose was paid a $2,000 a month retainer for 15 months beginning in the fall of 1984. Hillary was listed on Rose documents as the billing partner. McDougal remembers that Clinton asked him to hire Hillary one morning in the fall of 1984. The governor had been jogging, and McDougal remembers the incident because he was worried about Clinton sweating on his new leather chair. The arrangement was brought to light first by Jerry Brown during the 1992 presidential campaign, when he accused Hillary of a "conflict of interest." Hillary flatly denied that she had represented Madison before any regulatory agency.

By the time McDougal retained Hillary in 1984, a federal audit had already found "unsafe and unsound lending practices" by the thrift. Clinton's banking commissioner, Marlin D. Jackson, had warned him about the problems at Madison, but that did not prevent Clinton or his wife from helping McDougal.

In January 1985, Clinton appointed thirty-two-year-old Beverley Bassett as head of the Arkansas Securities Department, the state agency that oversaw S&Ls. Bassett had previously worked for a law firm that had represented Madison. She was a long-time Clinton supporter and a personal friend of Hillary's. Her brother, Woody Bassett, had been a Clinton associate since his days as a law student with Bill and Hillary.

On 4 April 1985, McDougal hosted a fundraiser for Bill Clinton to help retire a $50,000 campaign debt from the 1984 election. The event was held at Madison Guaranty, and it raised $35,000. Many of the checks were Madison cashier's checks, and investigators believe that many of them were fraudulent. In 1993 Ken Peacock, whose father had been on the board of Madison at one time, was surprised to learn that $3,000 had been given under his name to the Clinton campaign at the 1984 event. Peacock was a twenty-four-year-old college student at the time and denies that he ever made the contribution. There is every indication that McDougal simply used Madison funds, and names such as Peacock's, to divert money to Clinton. Donor records from the event have never been found. They were allegedly filed with Arkansas' secretary of state as required by state law, but if they were, they subsequently vanished.

Madison was kept open as Hillary represented the institution before the Arkansas Securities Department. She produced a report from a Little Rock auditing firm called Frost and Company that purported to show that the S&L was indeed healthy. Despite having no expertise or previous experience in banking or finance, Hillary went on to propose a rather novel approach to keep the S&L afloat. The bank would raise funds through selling non-voting preferred stock. The effect would be to raise capital without weakening McDougal's control. Charles Handley, the lead professional at the securities department's savings and loan division, opposed the plan. On 5 May, he wrote a note to Bassett suggesting that the plan was flawed, due to Madison's capital problem. Handley's assistant, Bill Brady, also advised against the proposal. Nonetheless, Bassett approved the plan. Her 14 May letter informing Rose of the official decision began with the salutation: "Dear Hillary." The plan to issue preferred stock never came to fruition. By the end of 1985, Madison was on the verge of collapse.

Throughout the controversy, the Clintons have implied that they were not close to McDougal. But, it appears that even in late 1985, McDougal and Clinton had frequent contact. On 10 December 1985, Clinton named McDougal to the Martin Luther King Holiday Commission. The following week, Clinton had dinner at the governor's mansion with Senator Fulbright and Jim McDougal.

In April of 1986, Susan McDougal obtained a $300,000 loan backed by the federal Small Business Administration. The loan was made by Capital Management Services, a federally sponsored lending company run by Municipal Judge David Hale, a Clinton appointee. The SBA loans are earmarked for the "socially and economically disadvantaged." Hale claims that he was pressured by Bill Clinton and Jim McDougal to make the illegal loan. Madison was about to be examined by federal regulators and needed cash to pump up the books.

Hale claims that he met Clinton on two different occasions to discuss the loan. The first was outside the Capitol building, when Clinton asked Hale, "David, are you going to be able to help Jim and me out?" Clinton's bodyguard, State Trooper L.D. Brown, remembers Clinton saying, "David, you're gonna have to help us out. We need to raise some money." Bill Clinton denies ever meeting with, or discussing this loan with Hale, and has gone to great lengths to discredit the man he appointed to a judgeship.

On 3 April, Hale wrote a check for $300,000 to "Susan McDougal, d/b/a Master Marketing." Where all of the money ended up is not known. What is known is that

$110,000 was put into the McDougal/Clinton Whitewater account. The $300,000 loan was never paid back. On the morning of 14 July 1993, the FBI issued a search warrant for Hale's Little Rock office. On the list of items to be searched for were the files from the 1986 loan to Susan McDougal and Master Marketing. White House Associate Counsel Vincent Foster received a phone call from the Rose Law Firm shortly after the search warrant was issued and allegedly committed suicide later that day.

The Arkansas Securities Department ultimately took no action against Madison. In 1987, federal regulators finally closed it down at a cost to the taxpayers of $47 million. This process was being repeated in a number of other cities where corrupt bankers, lawyers, and politicians were looting savings and loans. The opportunity for criminality on such a grand scale was made possible by a 1980 change in federal law increasing the size of deposits the government would insure, shifting the risk of bad loans from the banks to the federal government.

Bank officials made loans to friends, and to each other, knowing they would never be paid back, and that the taxpayer would automatically cover the bank's loss. Often, origination and other upfront fees would be charged and paid out of the proceeds of the loan. This was precisely the pattern at Madison.

A 1,050-acre development south of Little Rock called Castle Grande cost taxpayers $3.8 million. Federal regulators would later conclude that it was a series of "sham" and "fictitious" transactions between Madison insiders like McDougal and Seth Ward, Webster Hubbell's father-in-law. The Rose billing records, which mysteriously appeared in the White House in early 1996, showed that Hillary had done significant legal work on the deal. Prior to their "discovery," Hillary flatly denied she had ever worked on Castle Grande. When the records detailed fourteen separate telephone conferences or meetings between Seth Ward and Hillary during 1985 and 1986, Hillary revised her defense to claim that her work was "minimal" and "less than an hour a week." How much time Hillary actually spent on the project is beside the point. Any intelligent person even remotely familiar with the specifics would have to conclude that the deal was a multimillion dollar criminal fraud.

But, that was not the end of the Madison story. Almost unbelievably, the Federal Deposit Insurance Corporation (FDIC) hired the Rose firm to assist in the cleanup of the failed savings and loan. The FDIC, which was on the hook for the bad loans, sued Frost and Company, the auditors who misrepresented Madison's health in 1985. In other words, the federal government hired the Rose firm to pursue a case of massive fraud that its lawyers had helped engineer in the first place.

At no time did any Rose partner or lawyer tell the FDIC that they had previously represented Madison. Nor was it disclosed that Hillary had used the questionable Frost audit in her pleas to keep Madison open. The legal work was solicited by Vincent Foster in carefully worded, misleading language: "The firm does not represent any savings-and-loan association in state or on any federal regulatory matters." He used the present tense and failed to mention Hillary's past work for Madison. The civil fraud case was settled for $1 million, of which Rose grabbed $400,000 in fees. Web Hubbell handled the case for Rose and never bothered to mention yet another conflict of interest, namely that Seth Ward was his father-in-law. In August of 1990, Frost and Company gave $1,000 to Bill Clinton's reelection campaign.

To the extent that these events became known during the 1992 campaign, they were lost in a blizzard of denials and obfuscations. The corrupt character of the Rose firm under the Hubbell/Foster/Hillary troika was not well understood until the Robert Fiske and Kenneth Starr investigations, congressional hearings in 1995 and 1996, and the 1994 Hubbell criminal conviction. During an August 1995 hearing, House Banking Committee Chairman Jim Leach (R-IA) stated, "This could be described as an insider firm reaping profits from the public after insiders had defrauded the public and caused a loss to taxpayers." Rose would find no defenders on the other side of the aisle. Massachusetts Democrat Joe Kennedy concluded, "It's obviously a corrupt firm."

After originally denying that she represented Madison at all, Hillary adopted a fall back position once in the White House. She claimed that, although she had represented Madison, it was not a conflict of interest, an assertion discredited even by legal experts sympathetic to her politics. Harvard law professor Alan Dershowitz has pointed out that Hillary's 1984 representation of Madison could have had serious consequences for Rose. He wrote in 1994, "There is the potential exposure of the Rose firm to massive civil liability if it helped to cover up Madison's shaky financial condition. In recent years, both accounting and law firms have been held liable for failure to disclose adverse financial information about which it knew or should have known."

Alan Dershowitz used the Clintons and the Rose firm as a case study in his legal ethics course at Harvard in the spring of 1994. "My nose as a legal professor smells something suspicious in the activities of the Rose Firm," Dershowitz said. "It is the kind of elite insensitivity that Harvard and Yale and other elite law school students should be particularly sensitive about." He wrote, "There can be little doubt that clients sought out Hillary Rodham Clinton precisely because her husband was the governor. . . . [Her] practice of law was so close to her husband's base of influence that many will ask the question, just how good a lawyer Mrs. Clinton really would have been if her husband had not been the governor?"

Seven

Hillary the Activist

Ed Pickett is retired from the army. When Hillary Rodham Clinton's face comes on the television screen, he cringes and thinks of his dead son, David.

It all started with the return of a routine U.S. Army helicopter flight from Honduras to San Salvador during the first week of 1991. The chopper was hit with a barrage of small arms fire, sheared off a treetop, and crash-landed tail-first near the hamlet of Lolotique, in eastern El Salvador. A small group of Communist guerrillas, members of the Farabundo Marti National Liberation Front (FMLN), scurried to the scene, excited by their good luck in bringing down the chopper with nothing but their light arms.

The UH-1 Huey was a tangled wreck. The pilot, Chief Warrant Officer Daniel S. Scott, was dead due to injuries to the chest and neck. The two other men aboard were injured, but very much alive as they crawled from the wreckage. Lt. Col. David Pickett asked for some water. He never received it. He watched as Pfc. Earnest G. Dawson was executed on the spot with a single shot to the back of the head. Pickett tried to bolt, but was immediately hit with ten rounds, four of which were to the head and the face.

The loss was a shock to the Pickett family. The men were non-combatants and were not even based in El Salvador. David was married with three children and had seven brothers and sisters. Although the FMLN had tar-

geted American military personnel in the past, it had
never before murdered injured American prisoners, an
act in clear violation of the Geneva Conventions.

Ed Pickett is still pressing the American and Salvadoran governments to see that his son's murderers are
brought to justice. He is not only bitter at the FMLN, but
also at its supporters and apologists in the United States.
Pickett makes the case that pro-FMLN activists in the
United States prolonged the war in El Salvador. He holds
them responsible for the events that led to his son's death.

One American who helped the FMLN is Hillary
Rodham Clinton. She chaired something called the New
World Foundation (NWF) when it made a five-thousand-
dollar grant to the education fund of the FMLN's American support group, the Committee in Solidarity with the
People of El Salvador (CISPES). Pickett says, "I am sure
that Hillary Rodham Clinton will argue that the NWF
provided funds to support efforts on behalf of the Salvadoran sick and poor. She had to know differently!"

The Communist FMLN, supplied by the Soviet Union
and Cuba, fought the American-backed Salvadoran government for over a decade before laying down its arms
as part of a 1993 peace agreement.

Prior to the collapse of the FMLN's Soviet patrons,
left-wing groups in the United States and Europe romanticized the FMLN, mobilized opposition to American
policy, and raised money for the guerrilla army.

The First Lady of Arkansas was one of the most respectable figures ever to be identified with CISPES. But,
is it unfair for critics like Ed Pickett to seize on a single
foundation grant as evidence that Hillary supported ter-
rorism? An objective review of all her advocacy activities
is necessary, beginning with her Yale Law School days.

Hillary's immersion in left-wing politics came early.
As mentioned in an earlier chapter, she spent the summer of 1971 in Oakland, California, as an intern in the
law offices of Robert Treuhaft, a long-time Communist
and the husband of British-born Communist Jessica

Mitford. Treuhaft had been recommended to her by professors at Yale.

Hillary's involvement with radical lawyers continued at Yale Law School while working at the New Haven Legal Assistance Association. She remained involved with the burgeoning legal services movement through the seventies, working with several existing programs in Arkansas and founding Northwest Arkansas Legal Services. In 1978, she was appointed by Jimmy Carter as chairman of the Legal Services Corporation, which annually dispenses hundreds of millions of dollars in federal funds to local grantees. The appointment was a favor to a fellow southern Democratic politician and a reward for the Clintons' 1976 campaign help.

Over the years, Hillary served as chairman of two other large national organizations, the Children's Defense Fund (CDF), which she became involved with while still at Yale, and the New World Foundation (NWF). Hillary's connection to both groups was through Marian Wright Edelman, the founder of CDF, whose husband Peter preceded Hillary as NWF chairman.

There is a common thread to these affiliations and many other less significant ones. All her activity served to build a countercultural activist network and present a radical challenge to American institutions. The organizations with which she affiliated were, and still are, important components of this network. Having its origins in the New Left, the "movement" began its long march through America's institutions in the late sixties. Because its goals were often too extreme to be achieved through the political process, lawyers were especially important.

Hillary's commitment to building a movement is articulated in the 1987-1988 NWF annual report in the jargon of an organizer. She writes of the "support and development of progressive activist organizations." NWF President Colin Greer describes "fortifying the broader movement for progressive change" through "agenda-building, stabilizing funding bases, and forging creative collaboration between legal advocates and community activists." A review of NWF grants from 1987-1988 shows that the group's mission was more extreme than "liberal." Hillary's movement had an ideological boundary much further to the Left.

For example, despite the fact that nearly half the members of Congress opposed military aid to El Salvador, virtually all steered clear of CISPES. It was widely and correctly recognized as a support group for Communists in El Salvador who sought to seize power from a democratically elected government by the force of arms. CISPES was founded in 1980 on a trip to the United States by Farid Handal, brother of El Salvador's Communist party head, Shafik Handal.

Although CISPES spokesmen responded with charges of "McCarthyism" to the accusation that the group was pro-Communist, even the most liberal members of Congress quickly came to know the real CISPES. Senators Christopher Dodd (D-CT) and John Kerry (D-MA), the two most vociferous Senate critics of U.S. policy, were tagged as "death squad Democrats" and their offices were sites of sit-ins. The New Haven, Connecticut, post office was spray painted with "SENATOR DODD BLOOD IS ON YOUR HANDS. STOP FUNDING WAR IN EL SALVADOR." Not only did CISPES supporters engage in this sort of vandalism, but its demonstrations in several cities turned violent.

Two NWF grants totaling fifty thousand dollars went to an equally strident opponent of U.S. policy in Central America, the education fund of the Coalition for a New Foreign Policy. The coalition was the organizer of an April 1987 "peace" rally in Washington, D.C. The event was denounced by the AFL-CIO as a "classic front" for pro-Soviet activities.

The New World Foundation gave the Christic Institute some twenty thousand dollars in 1988 "to combat the judicial harassment and repression of black activists." Christic is much more notorious, however, for its bizarre

1986 RICO lawsuit alleging that a "secret team" of former intelligence agents ran a thirty-year conspiracy encompassing the Kennedy assassinations, Watergate, and Iran-contra. Initially treated seriously by the media, the suit named as defendants Nicaraguan contra leaders, prominent contra supporters like Gen. John Singlaub (USA-Ret.) and Major Andy Messing (USA-Ret.), Latin drug traffickers, and anti-Castro Cubans. In 1988 the suit was thrown out of court, and in 1989 the Christics were assessed over $1 million in court-ordered sanctions for filing a frivolous lawsuit. By this time, the group and its flamboyant president, Daniel Sheehan, were widely dismissed as crackpots. Their antics were even too much for reliably left-wing publications like *Mother Jones* and *The Nation*, both of which ran critical articles.

A grant of twenty thousand dollars in 1987 went to the Center for Constitutional Rights, the vehicle for the activism of the nation's most infamous radical lawyer, William Kunstler, who died in 1995. Since he first burst on the scene as counsel for the Chicago Seven defendants charged with disrupting the 1968 Democratic National Convention, the long-haired Kunstler repeatedly offered his services to other radicals, both in the U.S. and abroad. In 1981, he defended the Black Liberation Army in a Brinks truck robbery case. During the eighties, he also unsuccessfully petitioned the West German government to represent the Baader-Meinhof Gang, the Marxist terrorist group responsible for dozens of murders and bombings. Most recently, he was counsel for the Islamic militants who bombed the World Trade Center in 1993.

Kunstler said in 1975, "The thing I'm most interested in is keeping people on the street who will forever alter the character of this country: the revolutionaries. . . . I'm really interested only in spending my talents and any assets I have to keep the revolutionaries functioning."

In 1987, a grant of fifteen thousand dollars went to yet another group of radical lawyers, the National Law-

yers Guild. Founded in the 1930s with the help of Stalin's
Comintern, it was identified by the House Committee on
Un-American Activities in 1961 as "the foremost legal
bulwark of the Communist Party." The NLG served as
the American affiliate of the so-called International Association of Democratic Lawyers, a group that, according
to a 1982 report released by Rep. Edward Boland (D-
MA), functioned as a "political action tool in support of
Soviet foreign policy goals and military strategy."

Hillary's official biography prepared by the '92 Clinton
campaign makes no mention of her stint as NWF chair,
despite the fact that she oversaw some $23 million in
foundation assets. A few journalists, like Dan Wattenberg
of *The American Spectator*, did report on the NWF grants
during the summer of 1992, but the major media paid
almost no attention. There was no need for Hillary to
defend herself.

To be sure, not all the money went to out-and-out
extremists. NWF handed out $1.9 million in grants in
1987 and $1.3 million in 1988. Recipients included groups
like the NAACP Legal Defense and Education Fund.
Could it be that Hillary was simply not aware of the
character of some grantees? Could it be that she was
unaware that they received NWF money at all?

The available evidence strongly suggests otherwise.
First of all, the grants to the likes of Sheehan and Kunstler
were among NWF's largest. Most of its other grants for
1987 and 1988 were much less, often in the $1,000 to
$3,000 range. Hillary would have known about the larger
grants through simple attendance at a board meeting.
Secondly, Hillary is a hands-on manager with, as her
supporters boast, a grasp of detail. The NWF chairmanship was not an honorary post, and her relationship with
NWF was more than fleeting. She had served on the
board since the early eighties, and she was thoroughly
familiar with the workings of the organization.

Further light is shed on Hillary's relationship with
the pro-Soviet Left in a remarkable exchange of corre-

spondence that occurred shortly after the 1992 election. Rick Best, executive director of the National Lawyer's Guild, sent Hillary a clipping of an editorial from the *New York Post* entitled "Bill Clinton's Hillary Problem," which cites the NWF grant to the National Lawyers Guild. The "Dear Hillary" cover letter to the clipping reads in part:

> I wanted to send you a copy of the Post article. I thought I better not correspond with you during the campaign. It was a major effort to make sure that the NLG did not publicly endorse you. Don't you think that deserves a reward?

Hillary's "Dear Rick" response was so warm that NLG felt compelled to publish it in its spring of 1993 newsletter. The editor noted that he believed that it was the first letter from the White House to NLG since 1944. It reads:

> Thank you for your kind letter of congratulations, affirmation and support. Bill and I are filled with hope and enthusiasm as we face the enormous challenges and responsibilities ahead. We will appreciate your continuing support as the new Administration implements its agenda to get our country moving in the right direction again. Best Regards.

While the newsletter reveals NLG joy at having an ally in the White House (the Best letter makes no reference to Bill), it is not free of the disorientation experienced by the American Left following the collapse of communism.

NLG President-elect Peter Erlinder not only acknowledges this bewilderment, but also the Guild's pro-Soviet past:

> Who would have thought that the NLG would outlast the Soviet Union, socialism in China, the Guardian, and many of the organizations we defended and supported over the years. If the NLG

was ever the "legal bulwark of the Communist Party," it certainly was not a sufficient "bulwark" to prevent the Communist Party from disbanding. We have survived our most infamous client, but the struggle to transform our society is far from over. This is a politically confusing time and it will be a difficult time to find our way forward.

Hillary simply cannot argue that she was unfamiliar with the NLG and its goals. Indeed, as chairman of the Legal Services Corporation (LSC), she helped foster an explosion of left-wing legal activism, underwritten by the taxpayer. Most Americans are unaware that the radical Left's primary source of financial support is the federal government, and not its own cadre or even sympathetic foundations like NWF.

The Constitution guarantees free legal representation in criminal cases to people who cannot afford a lawyer. The ostensive purpose of LSC is to provide legal help to poor people in civil cases, a role played historically by local legal aid societies and bar associations.

LSC had its origins in the Office for Economic Opportunity (OEO), established as part of Lyndon Johnson's War on Poverty. His successor, Richard Nixon, vowed to veto any legislation creating a separate legal services agency. After liberal senators threatened to block funds for his Watergate-related legal expenses, a beleaguered Nixon signed the Legal Services Corporation Act of 1974 and resigned several days later. It was the last piece of legislation he signed into law.

Liberals wanted a federal role in legal services because of the opportunities it provided to promote their political agenda through the courts. With federal funding, legal services programs shifted from their traditional role of representing individual clients to developing a body of what became known as "poverty law," reflecting a class struggle ideology. Legal action became a tool to launch an all-out assault on the political, social, and economic institutions of the United States.

Clients were still important, however. For instance, a
poor person who had a problem with a utility bill might
unwittingly find himself as a plaintiff in a class-action suit
to stop the construction of a nuclear power plant. A client in a dispute with a landlord might prompt the local
LSC office to organize a rent strike. This taxpayer-spon-
sored activism made LSC controversial from the start.
Even liberal Sen. Dale Bumpers (D-AR) complained in
1980 that legal services lawyers "look for too many cases
which can effect an economic or social outcome."

When Hillary Rodham, as she then called herself,
was appointed to the LSC board of directors in 1978 by
Jimmy Carter, LSC had grown to a $200 million pro-
gram. As a former legal services organizer, she was thrilled
at the potential benefits to the "movement." She served
on the board from early 1978 to early 1982, and served
as chairman of the board for most of that time.

Her appointment created a little-noticed controversy
when it was submitted to the Senate for confirmation.
Hillary's successful efforts to expand legal services in
Arkansas meant an increase in litigation against individuals, businesses, and government bodies in the state.
As a result, more business was generated for Hillary's
Rose Law Firm, the state's preeminent firm. She was not
only building legal services, but also serving as a "rain-
maker" for the Rose firm.

Problems arose, however, in Hillary's answers to standard written questions provided to all the nominees by
Sen. Alan Cranston (D-CA). To Cranston's surprise, she
stated that neither she nor the Rose firm would refuse to
defend cases brought by legal services programs. In effect, she refused to recognize the conflict of interest of
serving on both sides of a case. Hillary clung to the
narrow distinction that, whereas such litigation was initiated by local programs, she served on the national LSC
governing board. Although she was confirmed by her
fellow Democrats in the Senate, the issue was still alive
two years later when Hillary's name was submitted for a

second term. She was again confirmed, but not before
her nomination was formally held up by the Senate Labor and Human Resources Committee.

One of her first acts as chairman was to oversee a
two-day board meeting and retreat at the posh Airlie
House in Virginia's hunt country to plot the future of the
legal services movement. LSC board member Mickey
Kantor, who in 1993 was appointed by President Clinton
as U.S. trade representative, argued that the goal for
LSC was to insure "access to power," defined as the re-
distribution of income and wealth in the United States.
Another board member, Steven Engleberg, pointed out
that such an agenda would frighten Congress and likely
not result in increased funding.

It was agreed that LSC must approach Congress on
the basis of providing lawyers to poor people. But, the
actual LSC goal would be to use the legal system to "em-
power" the poor. This was to be accomplished by ex-
panding the number of Americans receiving welfare, food
stamps, and Aid to Families with Dependent Children.
LSC was well suited to the task because of its unique
structure. It is an organizational hybrid insulated from
the supervision faced by other government agencies. Although the chairman and board are appointed by the
president, it is an independent, private, nonprofit corporation. Although it is funded by the federal government,
LSC employees are not subject to laws governing the
conduct of federal employees—not even the criminal ones!

This became a critical point for Hillary. During her
tenure as chairman, LSC became rife with illegality and
corruption. The Senate liberals, who had their way with
Nixon, gave some recognition to the danger that legal
services would get involved in partisan politics. In the
1974 law, they specifically forbade direct lobbying and
political organizing. Although loophole-ridden and difficult to enforce from the start, the prohibition became
absolutely meaningless with Hillary at the LSC helm, as
prohibited political activities flourished.

Although legal services work attracts its share of young attorneys who sincerely want to help the poor, left-wing activists dominate. The attitude of Geraldo Rivera, who worked as a legal services attorney in New York City prior to his talk show career, is perhaps typical. In his raunchy autobiography, Rivera describes preparing "mountains of ideologically motivated litigation" and brags, "We were tweaking the nose of the Nixon establishment and we loved it."

It is not known how many legal services attorneys are members of the National Lawyers Guild, but it is clear the number is substantial. According to a 1989 NLG newsletter, a survey of NLG members showed that out of a total of 6,440 active members, 17 percent were legal services workers. Thus, over 1,000 NLG members worked for legal services groups. Since these groups pay the "professional" dues of their attorneys, many taxpayers would be pained to know that they are the source of much of the Guild's income. (The same survey showed that despite NLG's claim to speak on behalf of minorities, only 3 percent of its membership was black.)

LSC provides no direct assistance to the needy, but serves as a check writer to the 300-plus legal organizations it funds. This includes not only local programs, but national advocacy groups, like the National Legal Aid and Defenders Association (NLADA). Unlike other attorneys, lawyers working for LSC grantees do not keep timesheets. There is not even a system in place to determine the cost of individual cases or categories of cases. Accountability is hindered further by the fact that, by law, only LSC itself may bring action against its grantees engaging in improper or illegal activities. Actually, LSC grantees have little restriction on what they may do with their grant money.

Hillary and her Airlie House allies exploited this opportunity with a vengeance, touching off a series of investigations and controversies that continued for years after her tenure ended. LSC grantees demonstrated a new boldness in pursuing blatantly political goals, and initiated some legal actions that can only be described as bizarre.

LSC groups in Illinois led a legal assault on the so-called Hyde Amendment, prohibiting federal funding of abortion. The challenges to the law were pursued all the way to the Supreme Court, despite President Carter's opposition to abortion funding.

At times, actions taken by LSC were truly outrageous. In three states, suits were filed to make the federal government pay for sex-change operations. In a Connecticut case, the suit also sought seven thousand to ten thousand dollars to relieve "frustration, depression, and anxiety" resulting from the "gender identity condition." California Rural Legal Assistance sued the University of California to stop research on agricultural productivity because it would benefit "a narrow group of agribusiness interests." The suit argued that farm machinery and other improvements deprived farm workers of their jobs. In Ann Arbor, Michigan, the school board was sued in an effort to require teachers to use "Black English" in teaching black students to read.

Hillary's LSC proved not only adept at promoting a variety of dubious social causes in the name of the poor, but also at building and financing the "movement" out of the taxpayers' pocket. In 1979, a Chicago LSC grantee filed a class-action suit against the Community Services Administration (CSA), another federal anti-poverty program. Congress had provided $200 million for emergency energy assistance to be distributed by CSA. Even in the face of dire predictions of poor people freezing to death, $18 million went unspent for the year. LSC sued CSA to get the money, allegedly for the poor.

The two "adversary" groups reached an out-of-court "settlement." The eight plaintiffs who had been recruited for the suit (three of whom later claimed they had no knowledge of it) received $250 each. The rest of the unspent $18 million went to fund pet projects of the two "adversaries" in the suit. The legal services groups that brought the suit received $3 million. The rest went for activities like promoting solar power.

Dire predictions that poor people would be denied access to the judicial system were similarly a staple of Chair Rodham's pleas to Congress for increased funding. At the same time, LSC grantees were carrying over vast sums of unspent funds from one year to the next. Between 1980 and 1982, an average of $46 million per year went unspent. Grantees were under no obligation to return the funds to the treasury, and they did not. A permanent legal services empire was being built.

In 1980, the empire was suddenly at risk. A tax revolt was in full swing. Movement leaders understood the threat to their redistributionist agenda posed by tax limitation. They understood that government could not redistribute what government could not take in the first place.

In California, a 1980 ballot initiative known as Proposition 9 would have slashed state income taxes in half. LSC responded by launching the Proposition 9 Task Force to fight the proposal. According to a 1993 General Accounting Office report, the campaign lasted three months and hundreds of taxpayer-supported lawyers devoted substantial amounts of their time to the campaign. The Western Center on Law and Poverty requested and received an emergency LSC "Special Needs" grant of $61,655 to hire four coordinators. Additional funds were expended by local LSC offices for "clerical staff, travel, printing and postage associated with campaign activities." The GAO report pointed out that the use of LSC funds for influencing ballot measures is flatly prohibited by law and that the task force's activities were illegal.

The real panic came, however, when Ronald Reagan defeated Jimmy Carter. Fearful that Reagan would seek reform of LSC, or abolish it outright, the LSC Survival Campaign was launched. The Proposition 9 Task Force was a mere warm-up in terms of illegality and abuse of tax dollars. LSC officials directed an extensive pro-LSC lobbying campaign, even though LSC is prohibited from lobbying. This activity cost millions of dollars and mobilized thousands of legal services lawyers nationally. LSC President Dan Bradley, who had been hired by Hillary, organized the effort. One of his subordinates, Alan Houseman, a former NLG member and leading legal services movement theoretician, supervised the campaign on a day-to-day basis.

Meeting only days after the 1980 election, over one hundred key LSC officials and staffers met at a luxury beach hotel in San Juan, Puerto Rico, to map plans for survival. Air fare alone cost taxpayers over one hundred thousand dollars. The campaign eventually included everything from political training sessions to the transfer of hundreds of thousands of LSC dollars to sympathetic outside organizations. Eight regional training sessions took place around the country, at which the attendees were addressed by Bradley and Houseman. The Denver session was captured on videotape. Alan Rader of the Western Center on Law and Poverty, fresh from his victory in defeating Proposition 9, stated that the legal services program had always been implicitly political and that it was time the participants became explicitly political. He asserted that the campaign "puts our attention where it ought to be: which is on the central arena in which the critical issues confronting our clients can be decided over the years—and that's the political arena, not the legal arena."

During this period, local LSC offices were advised to have their receptionists respond to poor people who called their offices with problems in this fashion: "I'm sorry but at this time we are unable to handle this kind of case. Due to the recent proposed federal cutbacks, we have had to reduce our caseload drastically. It would be unethical for us to take any cases."

The survival campaign continued unabated until early 1982 when the Reagan administration belatedly got around to replacing the Carter board. During the last days of the Rodham regime, millions of dollars were essentially looted from LSC coffers to continue the survival campaign. This frenzied giveaway was a part of the campaign known as "saving the rubies," a reference to Czar Nicholas sending the Russian Crown Jewels to Switzerland for safekeeping during the 1917 Bolshevik revolution.

An LSC grantee, the National Legal Aid and Defenders Association (NLADA), became the "corporation in exile." A yearly recipient of less than $100,000 in LSC support, NLADA received $2.2 million in late 1981. The grant contracts were most curious documents, waiving many of LSC's standard rights and NLADA's obligations. For instance, the requirements that NLADA abide by LSC guidelines and audit procedures were deleted. There were other things even more curious. Thousands of dollars worth of audio-visual equipment was simply moved from LSC offices to NLADA. LSC staff members responsible for awarding the grants went on the NLADA payroll upon leaving LSC.

During Senate hearings in 1983, LSC President Bradley admitted that Chair Rodham and the other LSC board members were repeatedly advised of, and updated on, the illegal survival campaign carried out by him, Houseman, and other LSC officials. For example, a 1981 Houseman memo detailing the campaign had been provided to the board. The board also asked for and received weekly updates on the "progress" of the effort. Thus, Hillary knew about the lobbying activities as a result of communications from the LSC staff. As chair, she had a binding legal duty to stop this illegal activity, yet did nothing about it.

There is no record of even mild disapproval by Hillary of Bradley, Houseman, or other LSC staffers. Indeed, several years later in 1986 and 1987, the Center for Law and Social Policy, headed by Alan Houseman, received two grants totaling $35,000 from the New World Foundation while Hillary was vice-chairman. The group promotes the same "poverty law" that Houseman tried to perpetrate at LSC.

When the Reagan-appointed board finally gained control of LSC, many of the files from the 1980 to 1982 period were missing, particularly those pertaining to the survival campaign. Documents had to be pieced together from copies obtained from LSC regional offices and individual programs. It was these documents that led to explosive oversight hearings conducted by the Senate Labor and Human Resources Committee chaired by Sen. Orrin Hatch (R-UT) in 1983. For the first time, the massive and unlawful scope of the survival campaign was exposed. Long-time legal services supporters were so defensive that Sen. Edward Kennedy (D-MA) stalked out of the hearing rather than sit through a viewing of a videotape of Rader's infamous Denver presentation.

Hatch concluded, "The political abuses by LSC and many of its grant recipients were not simply isolated anomalies. They were the business of Legal Services. They were committed on a national scale and were planned by key members of the LSC's national leadership."

Another committee member, Sen. Jeremiah Denton (R-AL), noted,

> The diversion of those funds meant that individual poor people were denied direct legal assistance which taxpayers assumed they were funding. These poor people with very real legal problems were turned away because their attorneys were too busy. Too busy doing what? Saving their own jobs. In refusing to perform their duty while performing illegal or improper acts, Legal Services lawyers have, in effect, robbed the poor.

A 1983 General Accounting Office investigation likewise concluded that the LSC survival campaign had violated the law, prompting a criminal investigation by the Justice Department. In July of 1984, a frustrated Assistant Attorney General Stephen S. Trott announced,

> The unauthorized activities of the Corporation, and
> many people associated with it, are uniquely rep-
> rehensible and beyond the scope of LSC's original
> mission. . . . Notwithstanding these inappropriate,
> misguided, and abusive activities, 18 U.S.C. Sec.
> 1913 as well as the federal theft and fraud laws—
> for technical reasons—were not violated by the
> lobbying activities involved here.

The "technical reasons" resulted from the way the
Legal Services Act was written. It provides no recourse
against those who violate the prohibitions on the use of
Legal Services funds. The Justice Department simply
lacked the authority to initiate criminal prosecutions.

Hillary and the LSC board and staff were almost all
lawyers. That did not prevent serious violations of the
law and a cover-up once the activities became known.
Most striking is the brazenness and shamelessness with
which the activities and the cover-up were pursued.

Rael Jean Isaac has identified "the bizarre 'ethic' of
the legal services attorney." In a 1985 book entitled *Legal
Services Corporation: Robber Barrons of the Poor*, published
by the Washington Legal Foundation, Isaac points out
that the ethic emanates from the self-perception of legal
services as a political movement to transform a system it
considers immoral, rather than as a vehicle for helping
individual poor clients. She quotes from an LSC training
manual: "Service to individual clients is provided only as
a means for winning the confidence of a poor
community. . . . The object of practicing poverty law must
be to organize poor people, rather than to solve their
legal problems."

Many of the LSC materials examined by Isaac were
published during Hillary's tenure as chairman. Nailing a
rat to an alderman's door, or seeking damaging personal
information on foes from "divorced or estranged spouses"
were suggested as effective tactics. In short, the perceived
virtue of the end, bringing down the system, justifies the
means.

Isaac summarizes this ethic:

> Whether an action is legal or illegal, ethical or
> unethical, becomes much less important than
> whether it will be effective in achieving an
> organization's goals. . . . In accordance with this
> strategy, numerous forms of unethical behavior are
> recommended in LSC materials; the law is treated
> as something to be bent out of recognition, if not
> wholly ignored.

On her way out the door, Hillary made a final hypocritical attempt to forestall Reaganite control of LSC. She
and several other Carter holdovers ran into federal court
and argued that since the new board members had not
been confirmed by the Senate, and were thus "recess"
appointments, they had no authority. In ruling against
Hillary, the judge noted that Hillary herself had joined
the board as a "recess" appointee four years earlier.

Despite being uncovered, the illegal LSC survival
campaign worked. The Reagan administration's attempt
to end federal funding stalled and failed, as did more
modest reform efforts later in the eighties. With LSC
funds pouring into almost every state and congressional
district in the country, local legal services operations
proved to be well organized and politically savvy constituencies. Additionally, LSC enjoyed the support of the
powerful American Bar Association. If the poor's legal
problems can be taken care of by the federal government, attorneys can dispense with their traditional obligations to support legal aid societies and to represent
poor clients for free.

On one of the few occasions during the 1992 campaign when Hillary was asked about her LSC stint, she
was unapologetic. To a *Washington Post* editorial board,
she invoked the needs of the poor and called legal services "a bedrock issue for equal justice and an absolute
imperative to have available. I don't think that it is liberal or conservative. I think it is how you make a justice

system work. I view it as a very pragmatic response to real people's needs."

A few days later, Hillary was the keynote speaker at an awards luncheon of the ABA's Commission on Women in the Profession. She told the well-to-do audience, "I encourage each and every one of you this year to become an active agent of political and social change." As the first chair of the commission formed in 1987, with award-recipient Anita Hill at her side, Hillary was in friendly territory. Indeed, she typified the well-heeled ABA functionary who fulfills her social responsibility by shifting it to the less affluent taxpayer. Her conscience is soothed by promoting political causes in the name of the poor, even if it is her own economic and professional class that is the actual beneficiary.

Popular resentment of the legal profession flared in 1991 when ABA President John Curtin, Jr., became one of the few people to ever lose a public confrontation with Vice President Dan Quayle. Following a Quayle speech which bluntly criticized the amount of litigation in American society, Curtin took to the podium and tried to lecture Quayle on the lawyer's role as guardian of the poor and powerless. The reaction was typified by Fred Barnes, a panelist on television's "McLaughlin Group," who pointed out that Curtin's last contact with a poor person was with the person who emptied his wastebasket.

If Hillary and other legal services activists unfairly used the poor as pawns to promote their social and political goals, as their critics charge, then she has been absolutely shameless in the exploitation of children. It is her activism "on behalf" of children for which she is best known.

Indeed, this activism has provided her with a desperately needed identity apart from her husband. She told *Vanity Fair* writer Leslie Bennetts in early 1994, "I was in public life separately from my husband, before I ever married my husband. I cared about issues affecting children and families since I was in high school." Of course,

Hillary got married shortly after graduating from law school and she wildly exaggerates the scope of her previous "public life." It consisted of a string of internships and junior staff positions. Nonetheless, it was during her early activism at Yale that she first met Children's Defense Fund founder Marian Wright Edelman, giving her a contact that paid off later.

In 1992, Hillary only half-jokingly said Edelman "kidnapped me for the Children's Defense Fund." Hillary worked as an intern with Edelman during the summer of 1970. After her 1973 graduation from Yale Law School, Hillary worked as a staff attorney for CDF in Cambridge, Massachusetts, until she joined the House impeachment committee in January of 1974. As the wife of a prominent politician, Hillary was advanced to leadership positions within the movement. She had remained in contact with Edelman, and when Bill became governor in 1978, Hillary was invited to serve on the CDF board of directors. She served as CDF chairman from 1986 to 1992, when she resigned because of the presidential campaign.

CDF directs its appeal to the trendy and politically correct. In star-studded Washington fund-raising events in 1989 and 1990, the theme was "Tell me a Story," and celebrities like Jon Voight, Garry Trudeau, and Susan Sarandon told their favorite anecdotes. Woody Allen sent his to be read. Allen was to later tell an interviewer in 1992 that he didn't see "any moral dilemma whatsoever" posed by his affair with his stepdaughter Soon-Yi.

Although Hillary served for six years as chairman, the Children's Defense Fund is more often identified with its founder, Marian Wright Edelman. She is a graduate of Yale Law School and was the first black woman admitted to the Mississippi bar. She directed the NAACP Legal Defense Fund office there from 1963 to 1967. In 1968 she founded the Washington Research Project, which became the Children's Defense Fund in 1972.

The racial turmoil of the sixties, including the assassination of Dr. Martin Luther King, Jr., and the riots that

followed, shook the American establishment. Corporate
and foundation boards pressured their executives to fund
civil rights and anti-poverty programs. Edelman had the
credentials and was well positioned to reap the benefits.
For instance, the Carnegie Corporation (which is actually
a foundation) provided some $3.2 million between 1970
and 1982 to projects she was involved with, including the
Washington Research Project.

Edelman has been successful in advancing her own
more extreme political agenda in the name of causes
that enjoy widespread support, such as fighting poverty,
civil rights, and the welfare of children. In 1968, she
figured prominently in the Poor People's Campaign, a
huge civil rights march on Washington. In her own words,
she spent the four months prior to the event in her well-
equipped Washington offices, "preparing papers for the
poor people to present to federal agencies and negotiating with those federal agencies for concessions on the
poor people's demands." In 1990, during the congressional fight over a sweeping national day-care bill, she
embarrassed her own allies in the Democratic leadership
by bringing children to Washington to lobby for the bill.
House Speaker Thomas Foley called her a "bully."

As early as 1971, Edelman saw the potential for advocacy in the name of children. According to a history of
Carnegie entitled *The Politics of Knowledge*, she told a
Carnegie staffer, "Child advocacy is going to be the next
big thing over the next ten years. . . . Children are the
unrecognized, neglected and mistreated minority in
America, much as the poor were prior to their 'discovery'
by Michael Harrington. . . . Children's rights may well provide the most promising vehicle for addressing broader
problems of poverty and race in this country."

How has the CDF addressed these "broader problems"? Mickey Kaus pointed out in the *New Republic* that
CDF attempts to reduce every public policy issue to "protecting children who cannot speak for themselves." Funding for federal programs like Women, Infants and Chil-

dren (WIC) and Head Start are not the only causes advanced by CDF in the name of children. CDF is also involved with an array of other issues, including taxation and defense spending, which are also pushed as "children's issues."

When it sticks to legitimate "children's issues," the inevitable CDF prescription is more government. For most of Hillary's tenure as chairman, CDF pushed for passage of a government subsidized and controlled child care system. This would have established a federally chartered day-care center monopoly. Congress instead passed legislation, signed by President Bush in 1990, that relied on tax credits to preserve for parents the choice of day-care at private institutions or at home.

With the ironic exception of abortion, an issue on which CDF takes no public stand, their agenda lines up with the rest of the liberal activist community. It is a member of the Alliance for Justice and the Leadership Conference on Civil Rights, groups that led the frenzied attacks on the Supreme Court nominations of Robert Bork and Clarence Thomas.

CDF's most revealing actions, however, come in the area of national security. CDF releases an annual critique of the defense budget and has, even during the height of the cold war, been at the forefront of efforts to drastically reduce defense spending. In coalition with groups like Greenpeace and Friends of the Earth, CDF launched a campaign to cut the defense budget by 50 percent.

Edelman is an advisor to the now anachronistic nuclear freeze group, SANE/FREEZE. Whether one views Edelman's concern for children as opportunistic or sincere, it is obvious that CDF has a far larger agenda than children. Clearly, it takes its role as part of a larger ideological movement very seriously.

Given her agenda, Edelman's embrace of children has insulated her from the kind of criticism she would normally receive. It has also produced accolades that have a familiar ring to them. On 8 October 1992, the

New York Times called Edelman "an impassioned and relentless champion of needy children and families."

At a triumphant CDF dinner in late November of
1992, Hillary gave her first post-election Washington
speech. She called Edelman her "mentor and leader"
and asked, "What on earth could be more important
than making sure every child has the chance to be born
healthy, to receive immunizations and health care as that
child grows to be stimulated and learn so a child can be
ready for school?"

Actress Glenn Close gushed to the *Washington Post*, "I
have such a huge sense of hope and relief that she is
going to be in the White House. . . . It is very emotional
for me. I have a 4 1/2-year-old daughter and I have
despaired over her future and the future of other children in this country because I thought it was being sold
out from under their feet. I feel a great commitment."

Washington Post columnist Mary McGrory wrote,
"Hillary Clinton is an advocate for children's rights, God
bless her. . . . Let's forget everything we heard about her
and greet the children's friend."

Hillary's mentor had taught her well. When she burst
upon the national scene in 1992, her advocacy for children became a recurrent theme in her defense to accusations of political extremism. (She might have also
learned about Washington's Sidwell Friends School from
her mentor. Despite all the talk about poor children,
Chelsea followed in the footsteps of at least one of
Edelman's sons in attending the exclusive, private academy.)

It is a good thing reporters did not challenge Hillary's
self-characterization as an advocate for children. If they
had gone back just one year, they could have reported
on an incredible double-irony. Legal services groups in
Arkansas filed suit against Bill Clinton alleging that Arkansas' child welfare system was in a state of crisis. The
suit detailed years of neglect of abused children and lax
supervision of foster care parents. Among the groups

filing the lawsuit were the Arkansas Advocates for Children and Families and Ozark Legal Services, two organizations that Hillary helped to found. William Grimm, an attorney for the National Center for Youth Law, which coordinated the lawsuit, acknowledged to *Mother Jones*, "There were many ironies here." Arkansas reporter John Brummett noted that while Hillary was traveling around the country moralizing on the needs of children, "basically, the state's child-welfare system was an abysmal failure."

As already noted, Hillary's profile was kept low during her first few years in Arkansas. Bill Clinton was not, of course, the first politician with national ambitions to have a "problem" wife. The strategy for dealing with it, however, might well be unprecedented. Other politicians have steered their wives into non-controversial causes like promoting the arts or highway beautification. Hillary, on the other hand, was encouraged in her activism.

As the wife of a political figure, Hillary advocated politically treacherous causes. Helping Communist guerrillas in El Salvador would have created a firestorm for the First Lady of any other state. It was the parochialism of Arkansas that provided Hillary the opportunities that were unavailable elsewhere. Unless it directly affects Arkansas, little connection is made between burning national and international issues and the votes of the state's Washington delegation. Witness J. William Fulbright, chairman of the Senate Foreign Relations Committee during the Vietnam War. His outspoken dovishness would not have been possible in any other southern state. It is not only ironic, but also telling, that the large national activist organizations championed by Hillary have little or no presence in the state to this day.

To the limited extent that Hillary's out-of-state activism was noticed, it was considered a political plus in Little Rock. Even if there was inattention to the exact nature of her activities, the fact that she rose to the top of organizations based in Washington, D.C. and New York

City was impressive enough in Arkansas, particularly to
local reporters.

Hillary's involvement in these national political net-
works was also an important, even indispensable, help to
the national ambitions entertained by Bill Clinton. The
last Arkansas governor to be noticed on the national
scene had been Orval Faubus, who hardly endeared himself to the East Coast media. Hillary helped Clinton to
establish liberal credentials and to network with potential
supporters among the interest group activists who played
such an influential and disproportionate role in the 1992
Democratic party nominating process.

It is remarkable that while Hillary was prominently
involved with groups considered out of the mainstream,
Bill played a large role in the 1985 founding of the
Democratic Leadership Council. This group of elected
Democratic officials sought to nudge the party back toward the center after the Mondale and Dukakis debacles.
Thus, the Clintons simultaneously ingratiated themselves
to both wings of the party. As a strategy, it might be
viewed as pure political genius. There can be no doubt
that Bill Clinton understood the importance of the doors
Hillary opened, but in reality, the strategy resulted more
from necessity than design, and it was not without its
dangers.

Bill was publicly dismissive in 1992 of his wife's al-
leged radicalism: "To portray her as some sort of left-
wing figure based on her activities over the past 10 or 15
years is patently absurd." But, it is obvious Bill was wary
of identification with the counterculture during his whole
political career. Discussing the McGovern loss with *Washington Post* reporter David Broder in 1980, he said, "What
was so disturbing to the average American voter was not
that he seemed so liberal on the war, but that the entire
movement seemed so unstable, irrational." The bottom
line was that as long as Arkansans remained oblivious to
Hillary's ideological pursuits, her activities posed no threat
to Clinton's political climb.

Most importantly, the trips to Washington, New York, and elsewhere allowed Hillary to get out of the state. For the same reasons that Bill and Hillary took separate vacations, Hillary's outside activities were essential to the survival of their political partnership. Hillary needed an escape from Little Rock on a regular basis. And, it gave Bill emotional breathing room and expanded the opportunities for his extramarital affairs.

Eight

Hillary the Issue

"I suppose I could have stayed home, baked cookies and had teas," Hillary defiantly replied to one in the throng of reporters on the cold Chicago sidewalk. It was 16 March 1992, and the wife of the Democratic front-runner explained, "But what I decided was to fulfill my profession, which I entered before my husband was in public life."

It was every political handler's nightmare. The candidate, or in this case, the candidate's wife, had already ignored the tugs of aides to break off the questioning. The questions were shouted, more like taunts. She had taken the bait. A few ill-chosen words would overtake the day's carefully planned message. The only justice in the situation was that no staffer was responsible. It was solely her doing. No underling could be humiliated or fired.

The safety of the rope line separating the candidate from the press was only a few feet away, but the damage had already been done. The *Washington Post* reported on its front page the next day that "Hillary Clinton stood defiant, feisty, and she said, confused." The article described her as "the defiant feminist" and recorded that the remark "caused aides to shudder."

The immediate cause of the outburst was an accusation on the eve of the Illinois and Michigan primaries by former California Gov. Jerry Brown that Clinton had steered state business to the Rose Law Firm. The accusation came just days after another rival, former Massachusetts Sen. Paul Tsongas, charged that the Clintons improperly benefited from a land deal, which he called the "S&L Caper," which later was to become known as Whitewater.

According to the *Post*,

> Through two months of adversity this winter, she never flinched, defending her husband in the face of charges of infidelity and evading the draft. Juggling career, family and political ambition, she seemed to embody a new generation of political spouse. But today she seemed unsure of herself as she answered questions about her role as the partner in Arkansas' biggest law firm and denied that she had benefited from the fact that her husband Bill is the state's governor.

It should have been a heady time for Hillary. The preceding week, the campaign had swept to victories across the South in the 10 March Super Tuesday primaries. The next day's Illinois and Michigan primaries on 17 March also resulted in Clinton wins, prompting Paul Tsongas to "suspend" his candidacy on 19 March.

The controversy was replaced on the front page three days later by the story of Bill playing a round of golf at the exclusive Country Club of Little Rock, which had never had a nonwhite member. Ironically, Clinton had been propelled to front-runner status on Super Tuesday largely as a result of the black vote, which he carried by a crushing margin of 82 percent to 8 percent over Tsongas.

On the heels of that story came the 29 March admission by Bill that he had experimented with marijuana at Oxford. What was remarkable was not the admission itself, but the Clintonesque formulation that he smoked, but did not inhale.

Although Brown upset Clinton in the Connecticut primary on 24 March, Clinton won the 7 April New York primary and effectively locked up the nomination.

That Clinton was still alive at all politically was nothing short of a political miracle. Either one of the twin crises that erupted just before the 18 February New Hampshire primary—over the draft and his infidelities—might have been fatal to any other campaign.

It was Hillary who saved the day in January when she pulled off the public relations coup of the entire campaign—the famous "60 Minutes" interview. Aired following the Super Bowl and seen by an estimated 34 million people, it was prompted by allegations of Gennifer Flowers, a former Arkansas state employee, of a twelve-year affair with Bill Clinton.

During the interview with Steve Kroft of CBS, Bill flatly denied any sexual relationship with Flowers, calling her a "friendly acquaintance." He seemed to confirm other infidelities, however, by saying, "You know, I have acknowledged wrongdoing. I have acknowledged causing pain in my marriage." Using the past tense, he suggested that such activity was a thing of the past.

Although Bill almost certainly lied about Flowers, he and Hillary nonetheless became the objects of sympathy, and there was extra sympathy for Hillary, the betrayed spouse. As she said, "There isn't a person watching this who would feel comfortable sitting on this couch detailing everything that ever went on in their life or their marriage." The spectacle had the feel of a Roman circus. Bill and Hillary were the persecuted, forced into the pit by the media.

Hillary's only on-air misstep came in her comment, "You know, I'm not sitting here, some little woman standing by my man like Tammy Wynette." Hillary apologized after receiving a note from Country music star Wynette which read, "Mrs. Clinton, you have offended every woman and man who love that song, several million in number. I believe you have offended every true country music fan and every person who has 'made it on their own' with no one to take them to the White House."

Far from persecutors, it was the media that saved Clinton. The importance of the "60 Minutes" interview was seen in a *Washington Post*/ABC News poll taken four days later on 29 January. Of those surveyed, 54 percent said that Clinton should withdraw from the race if it were found he had lied in denying an affair with Flowers. William Schneider, a political analyst from the American Enterprise Institute, told CNN, "The question is, is he lying? If that can be proved, I think as a political candidate, he probably has very little future."

The evidence is that Clinton did indeed lie, and the media chose to ignore it. Presented at a press conference the very day after the "60 Minutes" interview, the evidence was in the form of audio recordings of phone conversations between Clinton and Flowers that she said she recorded between December of 1990 and 16 January 1992, only days before she went public with her allegations. Clinton and Flowers can plainly be heard plotting to deny they had been intimate. Clinton even suggested that Flowers say she was previously "approached by a Republican" and asked to make the allegations, should she ever be confronted with them.

At one point, Flowers jokes about Clinton's proficiency at oral sex. The conversations were between two people who were more than "friendly acquaintances." Only once did Hillary have to respond to the contents of the tapes, and the probability that Clinton lied. It was on ABC's "Prime-Time Live" with Sam Donaldson on 30 January, and the exchange went this way:

> DONALDSON: If the transcript (of the audio tapes) is correct, she signs off a conversation by saying, "Goodbye, darling," and he says, "Goodbye, baby."
>
> HILLARY: Oh, that's not true. That's just not true.
>
> DONALDSON: That didn't happen?
>
> HILLARY: No, of course not.
>
> DONALDSON: Or he says, you know, "They don't have the pictures."

> HILLARY: Well, I'll tell you what. This was a woman who at least pretended that her life was ruined because somebody had alleged that she had a relationship at some point with Bill Clinton. Anybody who knows my husband knows that he bends over backwards to help people who are in trouble and is always willing to listen to their problems.

With the presidency on the line, Hillary was apparently more than willing to stand by her man. Her response to Donaldson fit a pattern followed by other Clintonites when confronted with damaging information during the campaign: deny everything and attack the messenger. Because the allegations had first been aired in *Star*, a supermarket tabloid, Flowers was an easy target. The fact that she had been paid an unspecified amount for her story was cited time and time again by the campaign. It was also the rationale cited by reporters for letting the story drop.

Albert Hunt of the *Wall Street Journal* called it a "shabby accusation" that "distorted and contaminated not only the political system but the judgment of some in the news media." Sidney Blumenthal, who only months before had obsessively pursued Anita Hill's accusations, contemptuously described Flowers as "the woman in red, trimmed in black to match the roots of her frosted hair." A *Washington Post* article asserted that her "body language" indicated she was lying. The indignation of Tom Oliphant, a columnist for *The Boston Globe,* led to open cheerleading: "That is why I am rooting like a fanatic for Bill and Hillary Clinton to prevail over a naked attempt by pornographers, learned thumb-suckers and go-along hacks to hijack democracy."

The most curious part of the media reaction, however, was to the audio tapes. Payment or no payment to Flowers, they provided a level of proof impossible to ignore. Yet, they were dismissed because the media said their authenticity could not be verified. There is no record of any major news organization seeking to prove or disprove the tapes. If the tapes were somehow counterfeit, there was undoubtedly a major scoop for the reporter who exposed the technical whizzes and/or impersonators who cooked them up. Strangely, no reporter went after that story. And, while the media was busy questioning whether the tapes were real, Bill Clinton was apologizing to New York Gov. Mario Cuomo for remarks on the tapes! Flowers is heard saying, "I wouldn't be surprised if he didn't have some Mafioso major connections." Clinton replies, "Well, he acts like one."

Hendrik Hertzberg, a pro-Clinton writer for the *New Republic*, admitted that very few in the press corps believed Clinton's denials of an affair with Flowers. Gary Hart, the former Colorado senator, whose own presidential bid in 1988 had imploded on the adultery issue, told the *New Yorker*, "They say Clinton handled his situation better than I did. Poppycock. It wasn't [Clinton's] decision to go on '60 Minutes.' It was an editorial decision not to pursue it any further."

Hillary also played a key role in the handling of the draft controversy. On 5 February, the *Wall Street Journal* reported that in the summer of 1969 Clinton had gained a crucial deferment from his draft board by enrolling in ROTC at the University of Arkansas for the fall of 1969, suggesting Clinton had been less than forthcoming on the circumstances surrounding his avoidance of military service. It had been an issue as early as the 1978 gubernatorial race, during which Clinton falsely claimed that he was never drafted.

Despite a two-hour interview with the commander of the program, Col. Eugene Holmes, Clinton did not tell him that he had already received an induction notice. Holmes said in 1992, "I believe he purposely deceived me, using the possibility of joining ROTC as a ploy to work with the draft board to delay his induction and get a new draft classification." His draft status was changed from A-1 to the protected category of 1-D, for students taking military training, but he broke his promise and did not report for ROTC, returning to Oxford for a second year. He reverted back to A-1 status on 30 October 1969, after a September announcement by President Nixon that there would be no more call-ups, when there was no chance he would ever be drafted.

Fuel was added to the fire a few days later by ABC News, which disclosed a 3 December 1969 letter of "apology" and "explanation" to the commander of the University of Arkansas ROTC, Col. Eugene Holmes, from Clinton explaining why he didn't report. The letter was written two days after the lottery, when Clinton's fear of being drafted was over. Clinton wrote of "loathing the military" and said he had "no interest" in ROTC, but enrolled "to protect myself from physical harm." Of finally subjecting himself to the draft lottery, Clinton explained, "I decided to accept the draft despite my political beliefs for one reason: to maintain my political viability within the system."

Where campaign staffers saw only disaster, Hillary saw an opportunity. She argued for her husband that the letter actually supported his previous statements that he had made himself available to the draft but was never drafted, a tact he took on ABC's "Nightline." Although the episode did not help Clinton, the fact that he faced the issue head-on stabilized the situation and allowed the campaign to survive.

Additional evidence that Clinton lied surfaced later in April of 1992, when Cliff Jackson, a Little Rock attorney who attended Oxford with Clinton, released personal letters from the spring of 1969 describing Clinton "feverishly trying to find a way to avoid entering the Army as a drafted private." The letters also referenced a draft notice, forcing Clinton to admit he had received an induction letter in April of 1969.

Even if these machinations had failed to save Clinton from the draft, it is still doubtful "he would have served and he would have served very well," as Hillary was to put it in July 1992. In September, the *Los Angeles Times* disclosed that Clinton's uncle, Ray Clinton, a politically well-connected Hot Springs car dealer, had successfully lobbied for a navy reserve assignment in the summer of 1968 in order to "buy time" with Clinton's draft board so he could attend Oxford. The reserve slot, for which Clinton did not report, was not in Arkansas, which had no available openings and long waiting lists, but was in New Orleans, where his uncle had friends, and was created especially for Clinton.

Although Hillary cannot be held responsible for every permutation of the deception surrounding Clinton's draft dodging, it is clear that she was willing to repeat key assertions which she was in a position to know were false; namely, that Clinton did not evade the draft and that he was not treated differently from anyone else.

By April, Hillary was no longer seen as campaign savior, but as an increasing liability, especially after yet another major gaffe. She was quoted by writer Gail Sheehy in the May issue of *Vanity Fair* repeating rumors of a sexual liaison between Vice President George Bush and a woman named Jennifer Fitzgerald, a member of his staff. Hillary blamed the "establishment" for "circling the wagons" in protecting Bush. One New York tabloid headline screamed "HILLARY'S REVENGE."

Hillary had let her guard down, and, again, was much too frank in the presence of journalists. She was venomous, albeit legalistic, in attacking Flowers: "If we'd been in front of a jury I'd say, 'Miss Flowers, isn't it true you were asked this by AP in June of 1990 and you said no? Weren't you asked by the *Arkansas Democrat* and you said no?' I mean, I would crucify her."

Although the May issue of *Vanity Fair* did not hit the streets until April, the outburst took place in January just after Hillary learned of the Gennifer Flowers tape recordings of conversations between Bill Clinton and Gennifer Flowers. Hillary was forced to apologize soon after the article appeared.

Trying to excuse her husband's sleaze by claiming Bush did the same thing was not only hypocritical, it was exceedingly unfair. The two situations were not comparable. In contrast to Clinton's own implicit admissions of adultery, the decade-old Bush rumor was denied by all parties and was previously investigated by several news organizations, including the *Washington Post*, the *Los Angeles Times* and Gannett News Service. *Washington Post* reporter Ann Devroy, who spent two months investigating the story for Gannett, called the allegation a "scam" and told the conservative weekly *Human Events*, "I looked into this ten years ago. I found nothing."

Most of all, however, the incident made Hillary seem just plain cruel. Grandmother Barbara Bush enjoyed a status with the public bordering on adulation. The impression that Hillary had viciously sought to inflict emotional trauma on the Bush family was devastating.

Hillary had fallen from the lofty position she enjoyed at the start of the campaign when she did nothing to discourage talk that she might be appointed White House chief of staff or to a cabinet post. At campaign fund raisers, she would most often speak of her own views in her own voice, as if she were the candidate. Less frequently did she refer to "we" or to her husband. She even bragged publicly, "If you vote for him, you get me."

By the time of the California primary on 2 June, Clinton had won the Democratic nomination, but his campaign was plagued with controversy, scandal, and Hillary. Many Democrats questioned whether the nomination was worth anything. A *Washington Post*/ABC poll the day of the California primary had Perot leading with 34 percent, Bush second with 31 percent, and Clinton in third place with 29 percent. Exit polls in California showed Clinton would have lost the Democratic primary 49 percent to 29 percent to Perot, had Perot's name been on the ballot.

Once the nomination was locked up, Hillary was muzzled and underwent a transformation, repeating a pattern from the 1982 Arkansas campaign. The writer Sally Quinn, a Clinton supporter, put it this way in the *Washington Post,*

> Suddenly Hillary was seen as tough, aggressive, angry, humorless, power hungry. And, stunned and bewildered by this portrayal, she went underground for a while emerging as a kinder, gentler Hillary. . . . She softened her hairdo, her clothes, her makeup. She steered clear of controversial issues. She appeared to be traveling more with her husband as helpmate, and her daughter Chelsea was suddenly conspicuous.

The physical makeover was accomplished with the help of two friends, Arkansas-born actress Mary Steenburgen and TV producer Linda Bloodworth-Thomason. Hillary spent the day of the California primary in June with three stylists they had recruited: Christophe for hair, Charlie Blackwell for makeup, and Cliff Chally for wardrobe. Christophe became notorious in May of 1993 as the stylist responsible for Bill Clinton's two hundred dollar haircut aboard *Air Force One* while it sat on the ground at Los Angeles International Airport, closing runways for an hour.

A philosophical makeover took place, too. In a late May interview with David Frost, Hillary rejected feminism, or at least "what that term has come to mean today." She continued, "I don't think feminism, as I understand the definition, implies the rejection of maternal values, nurturing children, caring about the men in your life."

She returned to her alma mater, Wellesley College, to give the commencement speech at graduation. She was not chosen by the students; rather, she was foisted on them by Wellesley President Nannerl O. Keohane. Graduating senior Gitano Garofalo wrote in the Wellesley *News,* "Ms. Clinton was selected and invited by administrators (such as Nan Keohane) in conjunction with only two seniors. There was no consultation whatsoever of the senior class as a whole. In fact Ms. Clinton was not even on the original list of nominees."

The *New York Times* headline read, "Back to College for an Image Makeover." Hillary Clinton was using the occasion not only to stump for her husband, but more importantly, she was using this political appearance in the friendly confines of her alma mater in a badly needed attempt to reshape her public image. In her speech, Hillary stated, "I could never have predicted, let alone believed, that I would fall in love with someone named Bill Clinton and follow my heart to a place called Arkansas."

"Why did she mention husband Bill in the speech?" queried Sarah Cashin of the Class of '92.

By the time the Democrats gathered in mid-July for their convention in New York City, Hillary's transformation was complete, and it helped head off another problem. Al Gore was selected as Bill's running mate, and Hillary suffered by comparison to his wife. Tipper Gore is a pretty, blonde, traditional mother and the quintessential political wife. Until the campaign, she was best known as a crusader against vulgar and suggestive rock lyrics, a brand of activism far different from Hillary's. As an organizer of the Parents Music Resource Center, and the author of a book entitled *Raising PG Kids in an X-Rated Society*, Tipper earned the enmity of rockers like the late Frank Zappa, who called her a "cultural terrorist." The transformed Hillary fit nicely as Tipper's sister-blonde. Of the new image for the Democratic ticket, *Washington Post* columnist Mary McGrory observed, "The two couples looked like people you would see coming through the hedges to your cookout, and everyone relaxed."

At the convention, Hillary behaved and stuck to the script. Another gaffe was to be avoided at all costs. Entering the convention, a *Washington Post*/ABC News poll showed Hillary was viewed favorably by 30 percent, unfavorably by 26 percent, and 44 percent had no opinion.

It was unprecedented in American politics for a nominee's wife to have an unfavorable rating nearly as high as her favorable. For instance, Barbara Bush registered 73 percent favorable and 14 percent unfavorable in the same poll. The sizable 44 percent no-opinion figure meant, however, that many Americans had not yet formed a complete opinion of Hillary, so the convention was an opportunity for redemption.

When she did address serious issues, Hillary stuck to the party line, even when the party line was based in deceit. When asked about Bill's draft record, she said, "Bill eventually decided to subject himself to the draft, but like thousands of others he was not called. He would have served and he would have served very well."

The media was not much interested, however, in Hillary's views on things like the draft. The "new" Hillary was on display and the media was happy to facilitate her "reintroduction" to the voters, as her aides called it. In the days leading up to the convention, she promoted her chocolate chip cookie recipe in a reader's choice bake-off between her and Barbara Bush, sponsored by *Family Circle* magazine. On her first day in New York City she proclaimed, "I want to have fun. I want to win the cookie bake-off." She joked to a tea arranged for congressional wives, "Try my cookies. I hope you like them, but like good Democrats vote for them anyway." Whether Hillary actually baked any cookies is not known. The cookies served at the tea were baked by the cook of a friend.

Hillary played the part of the all-American wife standing behind her husband. She told the *New York Times*, "I almost have to pinch myself to believe I am going to New York to see my husband nominated for the presidency of the United States" and "I am an old-fashioned patriot. I cry at Fourth of July when kids put crepe paper on their bicycle wheels, so this is, like, just incredible, it's so extraordinary to me." Republican consultant Roger Ailes commented, "Hillary Clinton in an apron is like Michael

Dukakis in a tank." It was even too much for some ad-
mirers like Judith Warner, who wrote, "Her wide-eyed,
down home comments were so extraordinarily hokey that
they sounded almost intentionally fake."

The evening Bill Clinton made his acceptance speech
in Madison Square Garden, Hillary wore a pastel yellow
silk suit. She even grabbed Tipper by the arm for a
dance, looking, as Bill put it, "like 1960s teenyboppers
recovering their lost youth."

Hillary's transformation coincided with a transformation in fortune for the Democrats. On the last day of the
convention, Ross Perot stunned the political world by
withdrawing from the race. Polls showed the Democratic
ticket opening a wide lead over the Republicans. Bill,
Hillary, Al, and Tipper embarked from New York on a
bus tour finishing in the Midwest, marred only by the
unceremonious ejection at a toll booth of a homeless
woman stowaway by the campaign whose slogan was "Putting People First."

Most of the coverage of the trip, however, was extremely positive. Jack Germond and Jules Witcover at-
tributed it to "the appearance and style of Clinton, Gore,
and their wives as much as the campaign rhetoric that
seemed to capture the small-town crowds and the hundreds who gathered at crossroads and other truck stops
along the way."

Hillary's new image did not make everyone happy.
Newsweek's Eleanor "Rodham" Clift, who later earned
recognition as Hillary's most shameless media apologist,
wrote, "Today's Hillary is a burned out, buttoned up
automaton compared with the vibrant woman who strode
purposefully on the national scene last January."

The Republicans were not prepared to buy into the
"new" Hillary either. She continued to be characterized
as a domineering feminist, and as Republican consultant
Ed Rollins had previously put it, "the yuppie wife from
hell." Bush/Quayle campaign official Mary Matalin was

interviewed beneath a Hillary photo which bore the scrawled inscription from the wicked witch of the *Wizard of Oz*, "I will get you my pretty, and your little dog too!"

Hillary continued to provide some ammunition. Try as she might to moderate her image, she could not simply walk away from her liberal comrades of so many years. Just before the Republican convention in mid-August, Hillary spoke at the American Bar Association luncheon honoring Anita Hill, whose allegations of sexual harassment almost derailed the Supreme Court nomination of Clarence Thomas. The fact that the public believed Thomas over Hill by a margin of two-to-one did not dissuade Hillary from praising Hill's "courageous testimony" or asserting, "All women who care about equality of opportunity, about integrity and morality in the workplace, are in Professor Anita Hill's debt." For good measure, she quoted Marian Wright Edelman, reiterated her support for abortion, and attacked "lectures from Washington about values." It is assumed Hillary was unaware of the 1991 incident that led former Arkansas state employee Paula Corbin Jones to file a 1994 lawsuit accusing her husband of sexual harassment.

Quayle, hoping to repeat his successful attack of the ABA of a year before, assailed Hillary and Hill, and charged the awards event made it "very clear that the ABA is just one more special interest group of the Democratic Party." Clinton responded to the renewed criticism of Hillary by adopting a more traditional posture as defender of his wife: "They don't have a vision for the future. So now they're trying to attack my wife. I feel sorry for them. I mean, it's just pitiful."

The skirmish was just a warm-up for the Republican National Convention in Houston, where the "family values" theme dominated. Articulated earlier in the year by Vice President Quayle and prompted by the decision of sit-com newsperson Candace Bergan to have an out-of-wedlock baby, the GOP embrace of the traditional family was aimed squarely at Hillary. Marilyn Quayle, in her speech asking for respect for homemakers equal to the respect accorded career women, became the anti-Hillary. A successful attorney in her own right, Mrs. Quayle said, "I came of age in a time of turbulent social change. Some of it was good, such as civil rights. Much of it was questionable. But, remember, not everyone demonstrated, dropped out, took drugs, joined in the sexual revolution or dodged the draft."

Several convention speakers repeated Hillary's 1991 "Elect one, get one free," promise, albeit in several different versions. Pat Buchanan seized on Hillary's law review comparison of marriage and the family to slavery and life on an Indian reservation.

Partisanship aside, the Republicans had plenty to go on in asserting Hillary's hostility to the traditional family. George Bush charged that his opponents "even encourage kids to hire lawyers and haul their parents into court." The evidence was in the form of three law review articles penned during the seventies on what Hillary called children's rights.

Even though during the convention the Republicans shot up in the polls, the damage to Clinton was limited by an extraordinary counteroffensive by a sympathetic media, which belittled the family values theme and grossly misrepresented what Hillary actually wrote.

The articles in question were written in 1973, 1977, and 1979. The first is entitled "Children Under the Law" and was published in the *Harvard Educational Review*. The second is actually a book review entitled "Children's Policies: Abandonment and Neglect," and was published in the *Yale Law Journal*, the same journal that published the third, an article entitled "Children's Rights: A Legal Perspective."

The articles are consistent in their viewpoint, appearing over the course of several years. None is lengthy and their content is unambiguous. The sum total of all three is fifty-two pages. A reporter could read and understand them in less than two hours. Many did not bother. Those who did ignored what they read, or deliberately misrepresented it. Dick Lehr of *The Boston Globe* claimed "a reading of the two key articles suggests that the GOP's take on Clinton's writings is word-twisting political rhetoric."

The point of the articles is simple and revolutionary. Hillary proposed to abolish the legal concept of childhood. Children would enjoy and exercise the same rights as adults. According to Hillary, "Many of the modern conflicts between parents and children arise because of the 'invention' of adolescence."

She further argued for the reversal of the presumption that children are incompetent to make decisions for themselves and that all legal rights granted to adults should be granted to children. These proposals would, of course, mean a radical and sweeping departure from present law, where children have limited rights, and special protections, until the age of majority.

One result would be the right of children to sue their parents, a prospect so silly that it was cited by Hillary's defenders as evidence that her views were being distorted.

The prospect, however, was not silly to Hillary. She proposed exactly that in the 1979 piece by asserting that "all procedural rights should be extended to children. They are entitled to legal representation in any proceeding in which their interests are at stake."

Her apologists hooted further at claims that this meant children and parents would litigate domestic differences, including household issues like taking out the garbage or using the car. They explained that Hillary was only suggesting lawsuits in extreme cases of abuse and neglect. They seized on the case of an eleven-year-old in Orlando, Florida, whose "divorce" of his abusive parents had received extensive publicity during the preceding July.

For example, Tamar Lewin, in a front-page *New York Times* piece entitled "Legal Scholars See Distortion in Attacks on Hillary Clinton," wrote that Hillary "favors

judicial intervention in only the most extreme cases."
Similarly, Jeffrey Birnbaum and Cathy Trost told readers
that Hillary supported such intervention only "in certain
extreme situations," in a *Wall Street Journal* story entitled
"GOP Targets Hillary Clinton's View on Family, But Some
Experts Cite Distortion of Her Position."

As evidence, both articles cited a passage from the
1979 piece:

> I prefer that intervention into an ongoing family
> be limited to decisions that could have long-term
> and possible irreparable effects if they were not
> resolved. Decisions about motherhood and abor-
> tion, schooling, cosmetic surgery, treatment of
> venereal disease, or employment and others where
> the decision or lack of one will significantly affect
> the child's future should not be made unilaterally
> by parents.

While the issues cited by Hillary are not trivial, they
do not fall into the category of "extreme," if that term
means they would be grounds for the child to sever relations with family. Far from exonerating Hillary, this
passage confirms that she did not confine the possibility
of litigation to "extreme" cases, generally understood to
involve abuse and neglect.

Further, and even more revealing in its omission from
both news articles, is the passage that follows in the same
1979 article. It reads: "In the field of children's rights,
we are not dealing primarily with existing legal rights
but with children's needs and interests and attempts to
transform these into enforceable rights. We are talking
about everything from compulsory school attendance to
driving privileges to nurturing requirements."

Although Hillary stated a preference in the first passage that household disputes not be litigated, it was a
preference only. In the second, she clearly foresees the
necessity of sometimes inserting attorneys between parent and child in disputes as mundane as driving privileges.

The second passage, which completely undercuts the premise of both the *Times* and *Journal* articles, was not quoted in either, demonstrating the newspapers' incredible bad faith, and typifying media coverage of the controversy. Margaret Carlson, in a lengthy *Time* magazine cover piece on Hillary, left it out in her dismissal of the issue in just two lines, "Rich Bond, the chairman of the Republican National Committee, caricatured Hillary as a lawsuit-mongering feminist who likened marriage to slavery and encouraged children to sue their parents. (She did no such thing.)"

The use of the Florida abuse case in the first place demonstrates the media's intention to deceive the public. Reporters ignored a prominent 1975 case from the period Hillary wrote her articles. A fifteen-year-old named Cynthia from Wisconsin sued to "divorce" her parents on the grounds of "incompatibility." There were no allegations of abuse or neglect. The girl just did not like her parents.

No one, including Republicans, ever suggested that a child should not be removed from abusive parents. It is a frequent and long-standing practice in every state in the nation. If Hillary did not intend to suggest something more extreme in her articles, there would have been no reason to write them. The Wisconsin case illustrated what she had in mind, but it was never mentioned once in the coverage.

The only concession Hillary herself makes to her own idiocy is that infants are indeed incapable of bringing lawsuits. She wrote,

> The first thing to be done is to reverse the presumption of incompetency and instead assume all individuals are competent until proven otherwise. It is not difficult to presume a newborn is incompetent, in the sense of exercising responsibilities and caring for himself or herself. It is more difficult, however, to prove a twelve-year-old totally

incompetent and I think impossible to presume
the typical sixteen-year-old incompetent.

Hillary's words were not distorted by being taken out
of context. In fact, they are more radical when cited in
context! When Pat Buchanan accused Hillary of believ-
ing that "12 year olds had the right to sue their parents,"
he was understating her views. She favored no such minimum age; she believes that all children regardless of age
should be considered competent, "until proven otherwise."

If these views are understood as they are written,
they seem ridiculous. How then, did they come to be put
forward by a woman thought to be so intelligent and
sophisticated? Is she simply too book smart? Perhaps
she's just the sort to invent a utopia that can only exist
in the pages of a law journal? The evidence suggests
otherwise.

Clues are offered in the law review articles themselves in her comments and asides on the family. Hillary
rejected the nuclear family unit with vehemence. While it
might seem extreme to some, this contempt would not
be considered unusual in the context of contemporary
feminism, or the cultural and ideological radicalism that
emerged from the late sixties.

Some of her hostility was expressed parenthetically
through the use of phrases like "fantasized family values"
and "consensus romanticism about the family." It was
also expressed directly. In 1973, she wrote, "The basic
rationale for depriving people of their rights in a depen-
dency relationship is that certain individuals are incapable or undeserving of the right to take care of
themselves. . . . Along with the family, past and present
examples of such arrangements include marriage, slavery, and the Indian reservation system."

This theme was repeated in 1979: "A curious thing
occurs when a society denies legal rights to certain citizens because they are thought incapable of or undeserving

of the right to take care of themselves . . . whether they be wives, welfare recipients, or Indians on reservations."

Hillary's articles might also be dismissed as theoretical meanderings if they were not also so consistent with the agenda of the "children's liberation" movement. Although never really influential, the movement surfaced in the 1970s, publishing books and newsletters, holding conferences, and litigating.

Hillary's writings are so similar to those of leading children's rights theoreticians that their originality must be questioned. She simply repeated points made by others, using nearly identical words. Virtually all her arguments and observations can be found in the 1974 book *Escape from Childhood* by John Holt, which was sort of a children's rights manifesto. Holt called childhood "as we know it, a modern invention," and in a chapter entitled "The Competence of Children," he proposed to abolish all legal distinctions between children and adults. Elsewhere, he likened the family to slavery.

A 1973 book entitled *The New Socialist Revolution* by Michael P. Lerner contained many of the same themes. "Childhood is an especially oppressive period," Lerner wrote, "accentuated by the economic and physical dependence of the child on his parents. Some of this is a result of the natural physical inequalities between children and adults. But much of it is the product of societal arrangements. Children are 'minors' under the law, without civil rights, the property of their parents."

In the book, Lerner also endorsed things like communism, the legitimacy of violence to achieve it, and the legalization of LSD. Lerner surfaced in 1993 as the First Lady's guru, and is credited as the architect of the "politics of meaning," the subject of a much-belittled commencement speech at the University of Texas during April of 1993.

The "kiddie libbers" should not be confused with other more numerous, self-styled children's advocates. Like Hillary, legal activist James H. Manahan was clear in stating their case. "I propose that we consider the logical and ultimate step—that all legal distinctions between children and adults be abolished." Hillary's CDF colleague, Patricia Wald, with whom she researched a chapter of a 1978 book, wrote in 1974 that children should vote. ("Many adolescents are astonishingly well-versed in politics.") Karen Adams of the National Child Rights Alliance asserted that kids should have the right to go to court as soon as they are able to talk: "We've had . . . children as young as three years old saying 'I don't want to live here anymore.' "

Of course, no three-year-old has yet figured out how to file a lawsuit. That is where the movement comes in. It proposes to counter the powers of parents with a whole system of adult children's defenders and advocates, who would be supported by the government. Hillary's affiliation with the Children's Defense Fund was no impediment to her suggestion that the group would be ideally suited to play a major role in this effort, a role which would undoubtedly result in millions of dollars in government contracts.

How the new system would work is outlined by Hillary's proposal for removing a child from a family, the ultimate challenge to parental authority. The present system, which she wrote is plagued by "adult perceptions and prejudices," would be replaced by new institutions, sure to be dominated by social activists. She wrote, "Alien values, usually middle class, are used to judge a family's child rearing practices. . . . Boards composed of citizens representing identifiable constituencies—racial, religious, ethnic, geographical—could make the initial decision regarding intervention or review judicial decisions. . . . The board membership should include parent and professional representatives, perhaps children as well."

The "kiddie libbers" themselves sometimes wondered aloud if ideas like this would be taken seriously. In the same article in which she proposed suffrage for kids, Patricia Wald acknowledged that the movement's pro-

posals appear "at first glance, far-fetched, wildly imprac-
tical, or simply woolyheaded." Despite this self-consciousness, no major news organization during the 1992 campaign accurately detailed the movement's philosophy, or
found it to be very controversial.

   To be sure, there were a few critics. *Boston Globe*
writer Thomas Palmer, Jr., quoted Carl E. Schneider of
the University of Michigan in a 16 August 1992 piece:
"The fact is once you transfer power out of the hands of
parents you're rather largely going to transfer it into the
hands of the state." He also found David G. Blankenhorn
of the Institute for American Values, who said, "I really
think this is of lawyers, by lawyers, and for lawyers."

   That is about as rough as it got. By focusing on legitimate, but less important issues, these experts might have
even helped obfuscate Hillary's weirdest views. Even when
journalists got close to the truth, it was still the Republicans who bore the brunt of the criticism. It took a September column assailing the GOP by John Leo of *U.S.
News & World Report* to acknowledge that he found some
surprises in Hillary's articles.

   Leo cited another obscure expert, Margaret O'Brien
Steinfels, the editor of *Commonweal*, who dismissed the
writings as "historically and sociologically naive" for
Hillary's assertion that "a boy or girl of fifteen who wished
to seek his or her fortune in the nineteenth century or
even more recently might have run off to sea or otherwise absented himself or herself from home without becoming a status offender or causing family disagreements
that could become legal problems."

   Leo wrote,

> In Clinton's pieces, functioning families are not
> organisms built around affection, restraint and
> sacrifice. They seem to be arbitrary collections of
> isolated rights bearers chafing to be set free. And
> there is no real indication in her writing that what
> children want and what they need are often quite

different.... In the world of public policy, the children's rights movement is still alive, but not thriving, largely because it is essentially irrelevant to the current crisis of the family. American children are not suffering from too much parental authority, but from far too little. Rich or poor, children are much more likely to be ignored and physically abandoned than they are to be "oppressed" by parental fascists.

Still, Leo concluded, "The Republican attempt to demonize Hillary Clinton is a shameful business."

Ultimately, it might have been the writings themselves that proved to be Hillary's best defense. They were so strange that most Americans simply did not believe they could have been written by an intelligent person. The Clinton campaign, for its part, did not repudiate the articles and never made a defense of them. It instead insisted Hillary's views had been taken out of context.

Although Hillary adopted a lower public profile, her influence behind the scenes was a powerful and divisive force in the campaign. Campaign strategists like James Carville, Paul Begala, and George Stephanopoulos, as well as pollster Stan Greenberg and media expert Mandy Grunwald, understood that Clinton's proclaimed centrism was the path to victory, even if neither they nor Clinton were philosophically wedded to it. The tumult of the campaign provided enough problems for the "war room" operatives without having to fight off boarding parties from the Left via Hillary's network, but they were forced to fight anyway.

One of the battles for campaign control was fought over, of all things, the location of campaign headquarters. Hillary's closest allies in the campaign, Susan Thomases and Harold Ickes, successfully sought to keep it in Little Rock where their influence could be maximized through Hillary. Once the nomination was in sight, Carville and company wanted to move the operation to

Washington, closer to the media nerve center, and where more experienced (and moderate) political hands were waiting to help.

Hillary's chief of staff during the campaign, Susan Thomases, is a close personal friend who served with her on the Children's Defense Fund board. Thomases is known for her extreme left-wing politics, assertive manner, and abrasive personality. Bob Woodward of the *Washington Post*, in his best-selling book *The Agenda*, described the magnitude of problems she created: "When Hillary's close friend, Susan Thomases, a New York lawyer, tried to push Gore out of the inner circle, Gore methodically moved to shore up his support. He met with everybody who might be relevant and never left the room when Clinton had an important meeting or discussion. He was relentless."

Harold Ickes, the son of FDR's political hatchet man and interior secretary, ran the New York primary campaign operation and the Democratic convention in New York City. Ickes was Jesse Jackson's campaign manager in 1988 and was despised by the campaign moderates. According to the *Wall Street Journal*,

> His friends still talk about the day he spewed a stream of obscenities at (the 1970) New York gubernatorial nominee Arthur Goldberg, whom Ickes considered a betrayer of the liberal cause. . . . Then there was the night in 1980 when Ickes halted the Democratic National Convention—for more than a half an hour, in prime time—because of a small procedural miscue between the forces of Jimmy Carter and those of Ickes' candidate, Ted Kennedy. And who could forget the time in 1973, during Bronx Borough President Herman Badillo's abortive run for mayor, when Ickes settled an argument with a Badillo operative by sinking his teeth in the poor fellow's leg?

After the inauguration, Ickes was passed over for an administration post in light of press reports that his law firm was under investigation for its representation of New York Local 100 of the Hotel and Restaurant Employees International Union, whose officials were allegedly controlled by two Mafia families.

Thomases and Ickes received a comeuppance of sorts in 1993 that no doubt pleased Carville and company. Remaining on the outside as lobbyists, Thomases and Ickes had their White House passes yanked in September of 1993, after the propriety of their access was questioned on the basis that it could benefit private clients. Carville, Begala, and Grunwald, who had also remained on the outside with private political clients, got to keep their passes. (One of Ickes' clients was Puerto Rico, from which he reportedly received ten thousand dollars per month. He helped preserve a multibillion-dollar subsidy for manufacturers, mainly drug companies, that Clinton had vowed to end during the campaign.)

After a year of delay, Ickes joined the White House staff to help promote Hillary's floundering health care plan, only to be presented with a subpoena from Whitewater Special Counsel Robert Fiske just weeks into the job.

Hillary also brought Mickey Kantor, her old LSC ally, into the campaign, but he clashed repeatedly with Carville, Begala, and Stephanopoulos. At the same time Clinton was campaigning against Washington lobbyists, Kantor was flaunting his campaign role in the pursuit of lucrative lobbying business for his law firm, Manatt, Phelps, Phillips and Kantor. On NBC's "Meet the Press" on 26 October, Kantor was forced to admit that he was briefing prospective clients on likely administration policies, but the media did little to pursue the story. The embarrassment Kantor courted was deeply resented within the campaign.

A few days after the election, Clinton faced what the *Washington Post* called "the first palace coup of his budding administration." During an initial transition meeting, the president-elect was asked to appoint Kantor as transition director, but Clinton balked. A furious political staff, already appalled at Kantor's selfishness, had not been consulted on the move, and were able to stop it. After the inauguration, Kantor was appointed U.S. Trade representative, although he had no particular expertise in trade. The job is an influence peddler's dream, and Manatt, Phelps busily signed up new trade clients, seemingly oblivious to the massive appearance of conflict of interest.

Severe tensions also resulted from the widespread rumor and belief that Bill carried on affairs after the "60 Minutes" interview, while the campaign was in full swing. Although they did not report on it, members of the press corps were also aware of frequent and bitter arguments between Bill and Hillary.

Christy Zercher, a flight attendant on the campaign plane, gave some idea of Clinton's compulsiveness, and the anxiety it must have produced for spouse and staff alike. She told the *Washington Post* that the candidate once startled her with a hug, and made comments like, "Oh, I could get lost in those blue eyes" and "You don't know what that outfit does to me." She also said that Bruce Lindsey, the Rose firm lawyer who functioned as Bill's personal fix-it man, instructed the campaign plane flight attendants not to accept invitations from Clinton to work out with him at the Little Rock YMCA.

On the day before the election, Rep. Guy Vander Jagt (R-MI), chairman of the National Republican Campaign Committee, accused the media of ignoring evidence of Clinton's continued affairs, such as a female reporter entering Clinton's room at 1:30 A.M. and leaving at 4 A.M. An openly frustrated Vander Jagt made the comments in response to a question in Omaha, but even this unusually direct assertion was ignored by the media.

Hillary put on a brave face, but the only possible result of Bill's recklessness was her humiliation. She had invested too much in him, and the prospect of becoming

First Lady was within sight. She had no choice but grin and bear it for the sake of the campaign.

On election day, exit polls showed Clinton would win a plurality in the three-way race. While staff members celebrated, Hillary paced, discounting the exit polls until the actual tallies came in. She remembered the exit polls in 1980 showing a Clinton victory, only to learn later in the evening that her husband had lost.

Bill Clinton received less than 43 percent of the vote, the lowest percentage of any presidential winner since Woodrow Wilson in 1912, and about what losing Democratic candidates received in 1968, 1972, 1980, 1984, and 1988. Only in Arkansas did Clinton receive a majority. At the same time, his home state voters were passing term limits by an even wider margin. Nonetheless, the media was ecstatic. Curtis Wilkie of *The Boston Globe,* in a page-one analysis the next morning, declared:

> Bill Clinton called for change, but he never dared ask for a mandate as sweeping as the one he received last night. . . . He piled up a popular vote nationwide that transcended predictions, while its party strengthened its hold on Congress. . . . The overwhelming margin of his victory gives Clinton an opportunity to create a new Democratic epoch, in the same way that Lyndon B. Johnson's 44-state majority in 1964 produced a Great Society.

In fact, Republicans picked up seats in Congress. Facts would not be allowed to get in the way of the media's euphoria.

We did it! Hillary's Inauguration Day hat drew negative reactions from friend and foe alike.

(AP/Wide World Photos)

Nine

Health Care

Calling it a tour de force would be an understatement. There she was, the First Lady of the United States with the media and the entire congressional leadership eating out of her hand. Flanked by Senators George Mitchell and Ted Kennedy in the Senate's Lyndon B. Johnson Conference Room, Hillary stood there as the only First Lady in history to confer with Congress on a crucial domestic policy issue. Only a week before on 25 January 1993, the new president announced that his wife would lead a task force to overhaul the nation's health care system.

With aide Ira Magaziner in tow, Hillary had met privately with Majority Leader Mitchell, a group of twenty-nine Democratic senators, Minority Leader Bob Dole, and a smaller group of Republicans. The meetings had not been an exchange, but an exercise in deference. Not even one of the Republicans offered a peep of discord. Mitchell said that the Senators "expressed their pleasure and gratitude at the First Lady's willingness to undertake this difficult mission." Hillary followed Senate Majority Leader George Mitchell to the microphone. As described by the *Washington Post*, she spoke "without appearing to take a breath" and with "grace and gravity."

It was the moment for which she had waited her entire life. Standing there in the glow of the TV lights with the world revolving around her was the ultimate in status. It was not only revenge over her husband and

185

every critic of the last two years, but also over every detractor and rival in her life.

A *Washington Post*/ABC News poll cast a bright glow, too. By a margin of better than two-to-one, Americans approved of her heading up the task force. The president himself was bogged down in an imbroglio over gays in the military. Hillary was already the administration's biggest asset and the media's biggest darling.

It was not a surprise when the media virtually ignored a story later in February by *Washington Times* reporter Paul Bedard that appeared under the headline, "First lady's task force broke law on secrecy." Bedard noted that reporters had been denied access to the first task force meeting. He went on to quote a number of attorneys and experts who asserted that this was in violation of something called the Federal Advisory Committee Act or FACA. The little-known law, on the books since 1972, applies when a president convenes a group of people, which includes private citizens, to advise him on a particular issue. Although the president is advised by all kinds of formal and informal bodies within his administration, FACA kicks in only when nongovernment employees or "outsiders" take part.

According to a litigation handbook published by the American Civil Liberties Union Foundation, FACA is "intended to protect against undue influence by special interest groups over government decision making." The law requires that meetings be open to the public and press, that advance notice of meetings be given, and other "sunshine" measures. The legal experts quoted by Bedard claimed that since Hillary was not a government employee—the First Lady does not receive a salary—her participation in the task force triggered FACA.

Liberal activist groups had filed a number of lawsuits under FACA during the preceding twelve years of Republican rule, most recently against Vice President Quayle's Competitiveness Council. Bedard reported that Public Citizen, founded by Ralph Nader, was "looking into the situation" with Hillary's task force, but ultimately no action was taken by the liberal groups. The issue had to be pressed by others.

Citing FACA, a doctor's group and two public interest groups wrote the task force and asked that their staff members be allowed to attend meetings. The response from White House Counsel Bernard Nussbaum asserted that FACA was never intended to apply to the First Lady and that the request was denied. The groups were encouraged to contact Nussbaum's deputy, Vincent Foster, should they "require further information." On 24 February 1993, Hillary and the six cabinet members serving on the task force were sued in U.S. District Court for the District of Columbia by three groups: the Association of American Physicians and Surgeons, the American Council for Health Care Reform, and the National Legal and Policy Center.

Some commentators accused the plaintiffs of nitpicking. Susan Trausch, a columnist for *The Boston Globe,* wrote, "Very few of us give a fat rat about the technicalities of a 1972 law regulating task force meetings. We do not care if she is operating as a federal employee, a private citizen, the president's wife, or all three. We just want a break on our health insurance." Others, including some liberals who had defended FACA in the past, were less flippant. For instance, the *New York Times* editorialized that the secrecy was "unseemly, possibly illegal and wrong."

The irony of the situation was apparent. Robert Pear of the *New York Times* reported that "Mrs. Clinton, a longtime supporter of liberal causes and 'public interest' law, might be hoist by her own petard," and quoted Peter Flaherty, National Legal and Policy Center (NLPC) president and coauthor of this book, on the issue: "The regime of openness in government has been built by a lot of people sympathetic to Hillary Clinton. Now she would just sweep away those statutes because they are inconvenient to her."

Flaherty was not only commenting on Hillary's apparent hypocrisy, but also on her unexpected reaction to the suit. Justice Department lawyers attacked not only the assertion that Hillary was a private citizen, but claimed that FACA was unconstitutional. They asked the judge to throw out both the lawsuit and the law. Liberals had never before attacked FACA, and this new administration posture was certainly curious. The response was obviously improvised, demonstrating that the White House did not take the lawsuit seriously. Neither Hillary nor task force director Ira Magaziner realized it, but this improvisation would come back to haunt them. By the time Hillary's health plan was dead, Magaziner was to find himself accused of perjury and his reputation on the verge of ruin.

An acquaintance of Bill's from his Oxford days and a close associate of Labor Secretary Robert Reich, Ira Magaziner is a six hundred dollar per hour management consultant from Rhode Island. He and Hillary worked together in 1990 on a national commission on workplace skills. In retrospect, he would seem a poor choice to direct the most important project of Clinton's first term. Magaziner had been associated with a string of public policy failures. But, there was a consistent theme in all of them that makes the choice less puzzling. They were grandiose in scale and involved a central role for the government.

A major mistake involving Magaziner occurred in 1989. Physicists have dreamed about cold fusion since the splitting of the atom in midcentury, but by the 1990s the possibility had become a running scientific joke. Yet to be achieved, cold fusion means the creation of atomic reaction from water, promising an inexpensive and nearly limitless source of energy. Researchers at the University of Utah grabbed headlines in March of 1989 by claiming they had achieved cold fusion in a test tube. The school's president said the discovery "ranks right up there with fire, with cultivation of plants, and with electricity." Non-

physicist Ira Magaziner was sold, too. He testified before
Congress in favor of a $25 million taxpayer subsidy for
the project. He warned that the Japanese were conduct-
ing cold fusion research and intoned, "If we fall behind
at the beginning, we may never catch up" and "I have
come here today to ask you to prevent another TV or
VCR or computerized machine tool or solar cell story."
Cold fusion at Utah turned out to be a hoax, the work of
overzealous scientists desperate for research dollars.

Magaziner spent much of the eighties obsessed with
"industrial policy," even as the governments in Eastern
Europe, which had practiced fifty years of industrial policy,
were crumbling. Industrial policy means government
action to direct investment toward economic activity
perceived to be desirable. In other words, a government
bureaucracy would pick companies to be winners and
losers, rather than the free market. Magaziner even tried
to make Rhode Island the guinea pig for the nation, by
coming up with a plan called the Greenhouse Compact.
Containing $250 million in new taxes to establish subsi-
dized zones or "greenhouses" for high-tech industries,
the voters instead smelled a rat and defeated the compact by a margin of four-to-one in 1984.

The frizzy-haired Magaziner, who says that watching
"Star Trek" on TV is his only diversion from work, was
attacked by critics like syndicated columnist Doug Bandow
as "divorced from reality." But, while many would believe
Magaziner guilty of dreaming too much, few would have
believed him capable of perjury. Ira Magaziner is a case
study of an otherwise respectable citizen who, under enormous professional pressure, discards personal ethics and
breaks the law.

In a 3 March 1993 deposition taken by the plaintiffs
in the lawsuit, Magaziner claimed that all participants in
the health care task force were government employees. It
was a falsehood, and it was not a small point. Even if the
courts ruled that Hillary's participation would not trigger
FACA, the presence of other "outsiders" would. Indeed,

the entire lawsuit might ride on that very question. It was a lie that stood for several months. Hillary and other participants in the task force knew it was a lie, but took no action to expose it or to correct the record. Nothing would be allowed to get in the way of drafting a health plan and getting it passed by Congress.

One week later on 10 March, Judge Lamberth ruled that the task force had to open its meetings to the plaintiffs and the media. This time, the media took notice and the judge's ruling was front-page news. The *New York Times* called the ruling a "rebuff to the President." *USA Today* reported it was "embarrassing." In reality, it was a split decision, and would have little impact on the operation of the task force. Lamberth ruled that the official members of the task force, meaning the First Lady and the cabinet secretaries who comprised its membership, could not meet in secret because Hillary was not a government employee. But, Lamberth also ruled that all the other people working on the plan who were organized into "sub-groups" could continue to work in secret, because FACA was never meant to apply to staff. Of course, Lamberth was relying on Magaziner's false representation that all the sub-group participants were government employees.

That evening on ABC's "Nightline," a debate between NLPC President Peter Flaherty and White House aide George Stephanopoulos was prefaced with footage of Hillary's triumphant trip to Capitol Hill. The ruling had exploded the larger issue lurking in the background, namely, Hillary's role in the White House. Flaherty commented that he thought members of Congress "were walking on eggshells" when Hillary was around. After some probing by Ted Koppel, Flaherty finally addressed the issue that members of Congress, including Republicans, had so far avoided. He said, "What a lot of Americans are worried about, Ted, is that we now have an American version of Imelda Marcos, wielding vast influence behind the scenes, with little accountability to the

American people." As they were leaving the "Nightline" set, Koppel chided Flaherty that the Imelda Marcos comparison was unduly harsh. For the denizens of the Washington media establishment, Hillary was still the toast of the town.

Lamberth's ruling was appealed by the White House and was overturned on 22 June, after the task force had supposedly already disbanded on 30 May. Justice Department lawyers argued that since Hillary "functions in both a legal and practical sense as part of the government," her participation in the task force should not trigger FACA. A three-judge panel of the U.S. Court of Appeals for the D.C. Circuit agreed. If it was a victory for Hillary, it was a Pyrrhic one. The appeals court also opened the door for the discovery of Ira Magaziner's lie. The plaintiffs had presented the appeals court with evidence that individuals representing a host of special interests had taken part in the working groups. The judges asked Judge Lamberth to go back and determine the composition of the working groups, a move which would give the plaintiffs access to task force documents.

Regardless of what the courts did, Hillary certainly lost the public relations battle on the secrecy issue. She repeatedly handed her critics ammunition. Rep. Gerald Solomon (R-NY) read into the congressional record a leaked list of over 500 task force participants. A similar list was published in the *Wall Street Journal* under the headline, "Do You Know These People?" Readers were invited to fax in any biographical information they might have. Finally, on 26 March 1993, the White House released a list of 511 members of the task force working groups, and their affiliations. All were government employees or somehow identified as such.

The *Washington Times* reported on 14 June that task force records were being shredded. An angry Judge Lamberth asked government lawyers for the name and address of the custodian of the records so he would know "who's going to be held in contempt" should they be destroyed.

On their editorial pages, the *Washington Times* and the *Wall Street Journal* were unmerciful. But, liberal newspapers editorialized against the secrecy, too. *USA Today* opined that it fed "public suspicion of government." Hillary's critics were eventually so successful in making the secrecy issue stick that in July of 1994 the *Washington Post* made reference to the "administration's secret Health Care Task Force" in a straight news article.

The health plan itself was supposed to be unveiled 30 May 1993 to meet the president's much-ballyhooed 100-day deadline, but it was not officially presented to Congress until 22 September 1993. The massive 1,342-page plan that finally emerged was the product of a complicated and gargantuan task force. Organized into 15 so-called Cluster Groups, 43 Working Groups, and 4 Subgroups, task force participants had to pass their work through seven "toll-gates" or check points set up by Magaziner. Hillary was told in a Magaziner memo that 1,100 separate decisions had to be made. She ignored outside warnings, however, that the process had become too lengthy and cumbersome, and that the emerging plan was becoming too complex.

The final plan was based on the concept of "managed competition" or "managed care." Individuals would all be grouped into purchasing cooperatives, or "alliances" as the administration billed them. The idea behind managed competition is to cut the cost of health care by negotiating on behalf of larger numbers of people. In this sense, it was hardly a new or revolutionary proposal. Health Maintenance Organizations and many other health providers have operated in this fashion for decades.

But, Hillary's plan went much further. First and foremost, it contained "universal coverage." Everyone would be covered, regardless of means, habits, or health. It also would impose price controls on providers, as well as centralized control over the whole system through a National Health Board. Worst of all, it contained a new payroll tax. The plan was sweeping and the government would dominate the new system. As the task force's own legal team put it in a memo to Magaziner, "There appears to be no precedent for the enactment and implementation of a national reform that alters so many existing statutory, administrative, contractual, private and moral arrangements as this reform would propose to do."

As preliminary versions of the Clinton plan were being leaked in early September, a trade association called the Health Insurance Association of America (HIAA) began running the now-famous "Harry and Louise" television advertisements. Two actors, portraying a middle class couple, sat around a kitchen table and expressed their fears that the plan could lead to rationing, a loss of choice of doctors, and a decrease in quality of care.

Hillary fought back and attacked the HIAA: "What you don't get told in the ad is that it is paid for by insurance companies. . . . It is time for you and for every American to stand up and say to the insurance industry: Enough is enough, we want our health system back." The Democratic party adopted a similar theme in ads rebutting the Harry and Louise ads that said, "The insurance companies may not like it, but the President didn't design it for them—he designed it for you."

What Hillary did not mention is that her plan had the strong support of the nation's largest insurance companies, who had helped develop it in the first place. The HIAA is made up of mostly small and medium-sized insurance companies, who stood to be squeezed out under Hillary's plan. The hypocrisy of the assault on the insurance industry was largely ignored by the media. It took the low circulation, left-wing magazine *The Nation* to accuse Hillary of "pseudo-populism." *The Nation* quoted Patrick Woodall of Public Citizen, a liberal advocacy group founded by Ralph Nader: "The managed competition-style plan the Clintons have chosen virtually guarantees that the five largest health insurance companies—Aetna,

Prudential, Met Life, Cigna, and The Travellers—will run the show in health care."

Another booster of the Clinton plan was the big drug companies, which had also come under rhetorical attack from the Clintons. Shortly after the task force was announced, Hillary had accused drug companies of "price-gouging" and "profiteering." Bill visited a health clinic in Arlington, Virginia, and asserted that pharmaceutical firms pursued "profits at the expense of our children." But, once the plan came into being, it contained new prescription coverage for 72 million people, translating into additional revenues of $10 billion annually. Pharmaceutical firms had not only been on the inside of the task force, but insured their access by hiring top Clinton associates as lobbyists. Johnson and Johnson utilized the Wexler Group, which included Betsey Wright, the keeper of Clinton's deepest secrets, and Bruce Fried, who headed the Clinton campaign's health advisory group.

While Hillary was decrying the Harry and Louise ads, which she would ultimately blame for the death of her plan, far more extensive efforts in support of her plan were underway. The HIAA would spend a total of $15 million on the thirty-second ads, an amount that paled beside the money spent by two giant foundations that favored managed care, the Robert Wood Johnson Foundation and the Henry J. Kaiser Family Foundation.

It would be an understatement to say the Johnson and Kaiser Foundations exerted vast influence over Hillary and her task force. Indeed, these two foundations were virtual sponsors of the task force. Most significantly, they provided the funding and cover for the secret and illegal participation of dozens of individuals in the task force. It was no surprise that Hillary's plan embodied exactly what Johnson and Kaiser had been pushing for years.

The Johnson and Kaiser Foundations are both liberal and specialize in health issues. They both were built on the fortunes of companies that stood to benefit enor-

mously from managed care. The Johnson Foundation
had assets in 1993 of some $3.4 billion, of which 58
percent was invested in Johnson and Johnson stock. The
same year, the Kaiser Foundation had assets of $446
million. In 1991, before anyone had heard of Hillary
Rodham Clinton, Kaiser announced a five-year, $100
million initiative to reform government health care programs. The Johnson Foundation had provided each of
twelve states with $800,000 in funding to draft health
care reform proposals, which ultimately were managed
care proposals. Johnson and Kaiser sought to replicate at
the national level what they had been sponsoring at the
state level.

In 1993, Johnson sponsored four high-profile "fo-
rums" on health care with Hillary as the centerpiece, and
a staff retreat for congressional staffers to which no Republican staffers were invited. Foundations are prohibited from promoting legislation and must be strictly
nonpartisan. The Johnson Foundation's activities resulted
in a terse letter of protest to Johnson President Steven
Schroeder from Republican congressional leaders Robert Dole and Robert Michel.

In June of 1993, Johnson purchased two hours of
prime television time on NBC for a special on health
care with Hillary as the featured guest. The cost was $2.5
million and another $1 million was spent on advertising
for the program. What was unusual about the show was
that it was not presented as a paid advertisement, like
the Harry and Louise ads, but as an NBC News Special.
For the first time in history, a major network had simply
rented out its air time, staff, logo, and credibility to a
special interest group. There were howls of protest, but
NBC News head Andrew Lack claimed that the Robert
Wood Johnson Foundation, and the program, had "no
political agenda." The Media Research Center of Alex-
andria, Virginia, noted that on-stage panelists leaned two-
to-one in favor of government dominated plans. Dr. Jane

Orient, executive director of the Association of American Physicians and Surgeons, one of the co-plaintiffs in the anti–task force lawsuit, called the program "propaganda" and pointed out that advocates of free market reform did not appear. The NBC special was only part of a $12 million media campaign by Johnson, which also included a $2.5 million effort run by Rock the Vote, a liberal group that had run ads on MTV during the 1992 campaign encouraging youth to register and vote.

The Kaiser Foundation sponsored its own $7 million dollar blitz in conjunction with the League of Women Voters. The ads claimed to offer "straight facts" on health care reform, but seemed to reiterate White House themes. Matt James, a Kaiser vice-president, claimed, "We are not pushing any side and we don't support any plan or proposal to reform the nation's health care." At the time, Kaiser was funding a column entitled "The Clinton Health Plan and You" in the *Washington Post*.

Meanwhile, Judge Lamberth's court was starting to pry loose task force documents and the litigants were poring over them. Not only did they show that the task force had twice as many participants as the 511 people claimed by the administration, but that many of them were not government employees at all, but lobbyists and private individuals representing a host of special interests. In court papers, the litigant's lawyer, Kent Brown, asserted, "It becomes clear that large, well-heeled, non-profit foundations invented this bureaucratic yet secretive means of achieving 'change' in the delivery of health care in the United States by directly influencing the government decision making process from the inside."

Most curious was the designation of some task force participants as "special government employees." The White House simply hired private individuals as temporary employees in an attempt to dodge FACA. Other ruses were evident, too, like an attempt to pass off five fellows of the Robert Wood Johnson Foundation as "full-

time government employees." These fellows were assigned
to Senate offices, but it was the Johnson Foundation that
paid their salaries.

The administration also claimed FACA did not apply
to consultants who didn't have an active role. One of
those consultants was Diane Rowland, a senior vice-president of the Kaiser Foundation. Secret Service records
show that she signed in and out of the White House two
days a week for several months. Another task force par-
ticipant was Lois Quam, a vice-president of United Health
Care Corporation, a for-profit managed care provider.

Quam's participation appeared to be a blatant conflict of interest because United Health Care stood to
financially benefit from the decisions of the task force,
not to mention the reams of inside information to which
Quam would become privy. It also helped fuel the controversy over a conflict of interest directly involving
Hillary. The Clintons were investors in a closely held
limited partnership called ValuelinePartners 1, which held
a block of United Health Care stock. The partnership
shorted a number of health related stocks, including
United Health Care. "Shorting" is the process by which
investors borrow money to buy shares to sell them at
current prices, in anticipation of replacing them at a
lower price. At the time of his death, deputy White House
Counsel Vincent Foster was in the process of putting the
Clintons' health care stocks into a blind trust, a task not
completed until 26 July 1994.

The documents revealed other participants with clear
conflicts of interest like David Eddy, an advisor to Kaiser
Permanente, and Robert Berenson, the president of
National Capital Preferred Provider Organization, another managed care provider. Neither Quam, Eddy, nor
Berenson ever obtained a waiver for any conflict of interest, as required by law. Eddy and Berenson also failed to
comply with federal law in meeting the thirty-day deadline for filing financial disclosure forms.

Every employee of the executive branch, including the "temporary government employees," are required to file a conflict of interest form within thirty days of beginning work for the government, either something known as a SF-278 or a SF-250. If a conflict might exist, the filer is required to obtain a waiver. Federal law prescribes up to five years in prison and up to five thousand dollars in fines for willful submission of a false or erroneous form.

Many task force participants filed nothing at all, or filed late. Ironically, the non-filers included every member of the Cluster Group called "Ethical Foundations of the New System." Most of the forms for the special government employees and the consultants were filled out in a different handwriting from the person signing the form. Some handwritten forms had a typed date beside the signature line, and some had a date typed over a different, whited-out date. At least five appear to have been back-dated.

Eventually, 250 boxes containing 500,000 documents would be released. Notable for what they contained, they were more notable for what they did not. While there are thousands of documents addressed to Hillary, there are virtually none from Hillary. This dearth of memos and directives is inconceivable. As implemented by Ira Magaziner, the process required Hillary's personal decision on thousands of details. There is no doubt such documents were withheld. Their release would have not only provided embarrassment to Hillary, but would have shed light on the nature of Hillary's involvement in Magaziner's falsehoods.

Did she direct Magaziner to falsely claim that all task force participants worked for the government? Or, did she become aware of Magaziner's lies only after they had been told?

It is a dubious proposition that Magaziner could have lied without Hillary's advance knowledge. The lawsuit against the task force had become, at the very least, a major irritant to the White House. Hillary had to be confronted with the problems it posed, and at the very least, she had a hand in the response.

Ira Magaziner is not a lawyer. His 3 March 1993 sworn declaration was in all likelihood prepared by a lawyer. The lawsuit was being defended by Justice Department lawyers who filed Magaziner's declaration. At the very least, they would have read it before submitting it. White House Counsel Bernard Nussbaum was probably aware of the contents of Magaziner's statement in advance, too. In a half-hearted defense, Magaziner relied on a claim that he cleared the statement with the White House counsel. The notion that Magaziner could have engaged in a single act of misconduct without the advance knowledge of anyone else is simply not credible.

Hillary, Nussbaum, and the Justice Department team handling the case were all lawyers. As members of the bar and officers of the Court, they had a responsibility to bring an instance of perjury to the attention of the Court if they became aware of it. None of them did, even though they were undoubtedly aware of it long before Judge Lamberth or anyone else outside the administration.

While Hillary must be considered culpable on this basis, any evaluation of her role in this matter must be much harsher. Her passivity in the face of Magaziner's lies is easy to prove. But, the circumstances suggest a far deeper involvement. Hillary called the shots on the health task force. It is unlikely that a score of prominent lawyers in two different executive departments would have acquiesced to Magaziner marching into federal court to make false statements. There had to be a greater force within the administration that they feared even more than putting their careers on the line.

In a February 1994 interview with Connie Bruck for a *New Yorker* article, Magaziner acknowledged that all the secrecy had been a mistake. He volunteered that the decision for a secret process was not his. When asked whose decision it was, he replied that he did not want "to point a finger."

Bruck concluded,

> It is hard to believe that this decision did not ema-
> nate from Hillary Clinton, although she may have
> found support for it from others. She had maxi-
> mum control of the structure; such a critical deci-
> sion would have been left to no one else. More-
> over, it was in keeping with her natural bent. She
> trusted few, and secrecy was a means of maintain-
> ing control; in Arkansas she had held back the
> revelation of the teacher test until late in the game.
> And her long-standing disdain for the press had
> not mellowed with her assumption of role of First
> Lady.

The secrecy and deception served its intended purpose to keep critics of the task force at bay until it was
too late to make any difference. Although the secrecy
forestalled scrutiny, it also allowed critics of the plan to
define it on their terms for the public. As the spring of
1993 turned into summer, Hillary's campaign for health
care reform lost momentum. Key arguments made by
the opponents were starting to take hold. Patients would
not be able to select their own doctors. Treatment would
be rationed. Old people would be denied certain operations if they were too expensive.

In August, Hillary joined a bus caravan called the
Health Security Express in what was supposed to be the
finale of the reform campaign. Instead, it became a
metaphor for its failure. Financed by $1.8 million pro-
vided by managed care interests, liberal groups, and
unions, buses set out from Portland, Oregon, for a twelve-
day, cross-country trip ending in the nation's capital.
Three other caravans set out from Boston, New Orleans,
and Arlington, Texas. Many of the six hundred riders
had serious illnesses and injuries, along with compelling
stories of problems in getting health coverage.

From the beginning, the caravans were like flypaper
for demonstrators who outnumbered Clinton supporters
at nearly every stop. The Republican party and groups

like Citizens for a Sound Economy and Ross Perot's
United We Stand America mobilized their local members. Rush Limbaugh took particular delight in announcing the location of caravan stops. Caravan organizers
canceled scheduled stops and arranged impromptu events
where no demonstrators—or positive media—could be
present.

Demonstrators weren't the only problem. As reported
in the *Washington Post*, "The riders endured overheated
buses, flat tires, blocked toilets. . . . Scheduling snafus
turned rigorous days into 16-hour on-the-road
nightmares. . . . Some suffered from heat exhaustion. One
was hospitalized overnight in Denver. Tempers got short."

The *Post* identified the "turning point" as a well-
publicized rally in Independence, Missouri, where Hillary
joined the caravan along with her husband and Al and
Tipper Gore: "After Independence, lunch stops turned
into shouting matches. Police escorts followed the busses
in and out of town." By the time the caravan reached
Washington, it had become "a public relations fiasco on
wheels," as Sen. Dan Coats (R-IN) put it.

For many of the riders, the worst was not over when
they arrived in Washington. While they were out on the
road, the president had signaled compromise on the "rock
solid principle" of universal coverage. Kidney transplant
patient Cathy Steen, thirty-eight, who had ridden all the
way from Oregon, learned that she would not be covered
regardless of what Congress passed.

As support for Hillary's overhaul of the health system
slipped, so did her prominence in promoting it. By the
end of summer, it was the president who was the central
figure in the debate. Congressional leaders introduced
their own reform measures to distance themselves from
Hillary. The House version retained the concept of universal coverage, but the Senate bill called for 95 percent
coverage by the year 2000. The president addressed the
National Governors Conference in Boston and suggested
that 95 percent coverage would be acceptable. In the

process, he undercut House allies and his own wife, touching off a firestorm of liberal protest. Clinton was forced to disavow his remarks the next day.

Congress never did vote on Hillary's health care overhaul or on any of the watered-down congressional versions. The votes could just not be found and congressional leaders put off consideration of any health care overhaul to 1994. It was put off again in 1994 as the elections approached. The promise proved to be false that health care reform would ensure a resurgence of liberalism and a permanent Democratic political majority. But, what accounted for the spectacular demise of an issue that was to establish Hillary as the most powerful woman in America's history?

Perhaps the best answer was provided by a former colleague of Ira Magaziner. Writing in the *Wall Street Journal*, management expert Michael Rothschild pointed out, "With initial public support well above 60%, nonstop campaigning by Hillary Clinton, and overwhelming support from the national media, the President should have been able to pass any reasonable health care bill. But what is reasonable inside Washington is no longer reasonable to the American people."

Rothschild opined,

> Beltway cognoscenti would have us believe that the American people were confused by campaign-style rhetoric and never understood the Clinton plan. But as town meetings, newspaper analyses, talk shows and congressional debates wore on, the American people figured out this much: Though Mr. Clinton promised a "simple" plan that would guarantee choice with security, he delivered a numbingly complicated 1,342 page plan that put another 14% of the economy under the control of federal bureaucrats.

> This approach to social reform—widely accepted just 25 years ago—no longer makes sense to an American public whose daily lives have been radi-

cally transformed by the first decades of the Information Age. Top-down social engineering by Washington's central planners is now intuitively rejected as an anachronism, a hopelessly inefficient throwback to the bygone era of the Machine Age. How did America's epochal transformation from a Machine Age to an Information Age economy affect the Clinton approach to health care reform? Apparently, not at all. The plan . . . reflects classic Machine Age thinking: Centralize decisions through monopoly power, ensure stability through tight controls, insist on a "one size fits all" standard and allow no room for local innovation. Plan everything out in advance—to the last nit-picking detail.

Newly released secret task force documents show that Hillary and Ira only feigned interest in proposals offered by the public, Congress, and even Administration officials. They had already made the crucial design decisions. This should come as no surprise. A complicated machine can't be designed by a democracy. To ensure that its parts will mesh, you hire the best engineer you can find, give him plenty of resources, let him work in secret, and announce the product when it is ready.

The task force allowed Magaziner the opportunity to live out his wildest dreams. He would design a new health care system for the country, and given such an opportunity, he would make it perfect. All it took was enough experts, enough meetings, enough memos. Because the pursuit of perfection is a noble task, the process had to be protected at all costs. The result was ethical lapses. Ultimately, Magaziner would escape criminal prosecution. It was not until late 1994, after key documents had been released, that Judge Lamberth realized Magaziner had lied. On 21 December, Lamberth asked Eric Holder, the federal prosecutor for the District of Columbia, to investigate Magaziner for perjury and criminal contempt of court. He also suggested that Attorney General Janet Reno should appoint an independent counsel to investigate.

The *New York Times* reported the next day that Lamberth's request sent "a wave of anxiety" through the White House. In preparation for a criminal investigation, Magaziner hired Charles Ruff, a four hundred dollar an hour attorney. Ironically, Ruff had been under consideration in 1993 for appointment as attorney general before his own ethics problems came to light. Like Zoe Baird and Kimba Wood, he had failed to pay taxes on the wages of his domestic helpers.

Reno announced on 3 March 1995 that she would not appoint an independent prosecutor. Judge Lamberth's request had been echoed by a majority of members of the House Judiciary Committee, who pointed out that the Justice Department, of which Holder's office was a part, could not conduct an impartial investigation because it had represented Magaziner in the original litigation. In her refusal, Reno claimed that Magaziner was not a "covered person" under the law by which independent prosecutors are appointed. But, the attorney general has the authority to appoint such a prosecutor anyway. Oliver North, for instance, was not a "covered person" under the law either, but he was investigated by just such a prosecutor in 1987. On 3 August 1995 Eric Holder announced that he would not prosecute Magaziner.

The plaintiffs accused the Clinton administration of a cover-up. Both Reno and Holder were appointed by Clinton, and Reno owed her job to Hillary. Additionally, the *Washington Post* reported in January of 1995 that Holder was under consideration by Clinton for appointment to a federal judgeship. If Justice Department lawyers had instructed Magaziner to lie, or were even aware of it, they might face criminal charges, as well. If there was ever a set of circumstances under which an independent counsel was necessary to ensure an impartial investigation, this was it.

Hillary's goals for the task force were different from Magaziner's. Whereas Magaziner sought perfection, Hillary sought power. The intricacies of the plan held no fascination for her. The fact that the plan would be hers did. For the first few months of 1993, Hillary experienced her dream. The attempt to restructure one-sixth of the nation's economy, and the initial belief that she would succeed, created an unprecedented perception of power. She enjoyed more status than any congressman, senator, governor, Supreme Court Justice, or even the president. Powerful men in charge of huge corporations hung on her every word. She dominated the media, and the coverage was fawning. Her critics, so aggressive during the 1992 campaign, couldn't do a thing.

In Washington the perception of power is power. Real power had never before been exercised by a First Lady. Therefore, Hillary was not only a powerful First Lady, but was to be a historic First Lady. In the year 2093, school children would open history books and might or might not read about President Clinton, but First Lady Hillary was going to be right there.

Like many dreams, however, Hillary's came to an end, dying along with her health care plan. The defeat was devastating. First, the purpose of the entire Clinton presidency seemed to evaporate because so much had been staked on its passage. Secondly, it destroyed the resurgent notion advanced by liberals in 1992 that Americans were ready for a return to activist government. The defeat emboldened conservatives in the 1994 elections, and Republicans gained control of both the House and the Senate. It was more than a personal defeat for Hillary. It was a turning point in American history, and Hillary found herself on the wrong side of the issue.

By 1995, the political agenda was being dominated by Republicans, especially by the new House Speaker, Newt Gingrich. President Clinton was forced to assert during a press conference that he was still "relevant."

Hillary made no such assertion about herself, and no one made it on her behalf. Her defeat was total and final. She would still wield influence on her husband and within the White House, but it would be exercised in a traditional way, in the manner of previous First Ladies. The new role she had pioneered, the independent and powerful First Lady with her own agenda and power base, was a thing of the past. The grand experiment, which created so much excitement in 1993, had failed.

Ten

Traditional Hillary

"So none of this happened?" the reporter asked. Bill Clinton stammered, "We . . . we did, if, the, the, I, I, the stories are just as they have been said." Finally, he mumbled, "They're outrageous, and they're not so."

Never had Hillary looked so uncomfortable. She sat a few feet from the president on a sofa amidst the decorations for Christmas of 1993. But emotionally, she had to be miles away. Allegations by two Arkansas state troopers that Bill had engaged in numerous extramarital affairs had just been published in *The American Spectator* and the *Los Angeles Times*. Clinton's denial was so halting and confused that it did everything but confirm the allegations. It would be played and repeated on every newscast across the country.

Unlike her firm demeanor on "60 Minutes" in 1992, which had saved the day, all Hillary could do this time was rise and offer Christmas cookies to reporters. As she roamed the room with a cookie tray, she lamely asserted, "I actually made some of these." In terms of her personal humiliation, nothing was worse—not "60 Minutes," not the "cookies and tea" remark on the sidewalk in Chicago, not even the defeat on health care.

The White House had done everything to avoid such a scene. Only reporters from the Arkansas media were invited for the Christmas interview. But, even these tame journalists could not ignore the trooper bombshell, and the president was asked the direct question. Ironically,

the controversy had been fueled by Hillary. The day
before, she lashed out, putting the story on the front
page of every newspaper in the country. Once again, she
was the good soldier. Once again, she was unwilling to
turn her public anger on her husband. Instead, she
blamed his political foes: "I find it not an accident that
every time he is on the verge of fulfilling his commitment to the American people and they are responding,
out comes yet another round of these outrageous, terrible stories that people plant for political and financial
reasons."

On 23 December 1993 all three network morning
shows had scheduled interviews with the First Lady on
Christmas at the White House. All three canceled when
the White House tried to stipulate that no questions
unrelated to Christmas be asked.

As if the trooper story was not bad enough, the White
House was also dodging questions about the removal of
Whitewater documents from Vincent Foster's office in
the wake of his death. At Hillary's insistence, the White
House had withheld the documents from the Justice
Department. Hillary lost this battle on 23 December when
Bill instructed his lawyer, David Kendall, to hand over
the documents, after arranging a protective subpoena
from the Justice Department. In other words, the Clintons
would hand over the papers, but they could not be made
public.

And then, in March, the cattle futures story broke.
The disclosure that Hillary made one hundred thousand
dollars on a one thousand dollar investment in ten months
in 1979 completed the public relations drubbing. Her
approval ratings dropped to an unprecedented low of 44
percent.

At a carefully orchestrated, "surprise" press conference on 22 April 1994 Hillary came out of hiding and
answered questions on her cattle profits and the filched
Whitewater documents. The event was held on a Friday
afternoon with the war in Bosnia escalating and Richard

Nixon only hours from death. It was held in the State Dining Room, under a large portrait of Honest Abe Lincoln. Mandy Grunwald, the Clintons' media consultant, dressed Hillary in a pink, feminine outfit. She was seated comfortably in a regal-looking chair by the fireplace, surrounded by ferns and flowers, which matched her pink outfit. Although the White House claimed that she had discussed the press conference only the night before with her husband, Hillary was well prepared for the event. She had been grilled at length by a team of trial lawyers from the prestigious Williams & Connolly firm, which specializes in defending corporate executives accused of white collar crimes.

"Pretty in Pink" was how many reporters led their stories. Gwen Ifill wrote in the *New York Times*, "Defending her friends and telling stories about her parents and daughter, the First Lady turned what could have been a bruising tell-all about the Whitewater inquiry into a fireside chat." The press conference was termed a "virtuoso performance" by the *San Francisco Examiner*. Connie Chung proclaimed on CBS, "This is a person who does not buckle under fire." Ted Koppel called it a "stunning performance."

But, syndicated columnist Tony Snow noted Hillary's new public persona. "Despite the planning, her performance fed every awful stereotype of women as mercurial, easily confused by numbers, dependent on big strong men and ditzy under pressure. Mrs. Clinton regularly portrayed herself as a rube from the hills and described past fibs and foibles as 'a result of our inexperience in Washington.'"

Gone was the pretense of the powerful, brilliant Hillary. At this press conference, she displayed a frequent loss of memory on most issues and a feigned unsophistication on various matters, including legal issues. She portrayed herself as an innocent female taking advice from Jim Blair and Jim McDougal. When asked whether she should "have questioned" Whitewater finances when she knew there was no cash flow, Hillary responded with the flippancy of a teen-ager, "Well, shoulda, coulda, woulda, we didn't." But, most of Hillary's responses were in fact very lawyerly in their evasion. "There's really no evidence of that." "I know of nothing to support that." "I can't answer that."

"Hillary the Warrior had metamorphosed into Hillary the Submissive, just as the proud Hillary Rodham had once been transformed into Mrs. Hillary Clinton," Leslie Bennetts wrote in *Vanity Fair*. "This is a woman who will, in the end, do whatever is necessary to achieve her goal, no matter how bitter the pill she must swallow."

In August of 1994, the Senate Banking Committee held hearings on Whitewater which demonstrated that Hillary had been dishonest about her role in the removal of documents from Vincent Foster's office. When asked about it in April, Hillary claimed that she could not "speak to that in any detail" and pointed out that she was in Arkansas at the time. As testimony by her Chief of Staff Maggie Williams showed, however, it was Hillary who had directed Williams to remove the papers. It is true that Hillary might not have known all the details of her aides' actions, but she conveniently failed to mention that they were acting at her direction by telephone. Michael Kramer put to paper in *Time* magazine what much of the White House press corps had already privately concluded: "No one yet knows why the Clintons appear to have ignored the lesson of Watergate: the cover-up is invariably worse than the matters the participants seek to conceal. What we do know, however, is that Mrs. Clinton is more like Mr. Clinton than anyone ever realized. Slick Willie, meet Slippery Hillary."

Amidst these problems, Hillary stayed out of the public eye. Her reemergence was slow and carefully orchestrated, and it was as Traditional First Lady. She told Ann Landers and other gossip columnists that she had been "naive and dumb" in her previous pursuits as First Lady. Hillary told Bridget Kendall of the BBC,

> I had a wonderful upbringing by my parents,
> schooling and church. Although my father had very
> strong beliefs, they were of a Republican Party that
> unfortunately seems to be vanishing in many parts
> of the country. He was conservative in the sense
> that he believed in conserving and investing to
> conserve. . . . So although he was a Republican and
> a conservative, those are values I still feel I hold.
> I believe strongly in the responsibility of individu-
> als. I happen to think that government can either
> impede or assist in individuals becoming more self-
> sufficient, and I don't see any contradiction in that.

Hillary told *Newsweek* that abortion was "wrong," and
that women should have abortions only after "the most
careful soul-searching." Hillary also claimed "a great deal
of sympathy" for fundamentalist Christians who, like her,
are often misunderstood.

Shortly thereafter, she condemned premarital sex and
said that young women should wait until marriage to
have sex.

In 1995, Hillary embarked on foreign tours of Asia
and Latin America. She was at her traditional best—so
much so that the *Calcutta Telegraph* newspaper lamented,
"For someone billed as one of the most able and sensi-
tized minds of the American administration, Mrs. Clinton
was singularly insensate and solely decorative today. . . . It
could just as well have been Lady Diana, Jane Fonda or
(Miss World) Aishwarya Rai speaking."

In Latin America, Hillary was asked about the Million Man March, featuring Louis Farrakahan of the Nation of Islam, which had taken place the previous day.
She suggested that reporters refer to her husband's remarks for an answer. When asked about her role in the
upcoming reelection campaign, she replied that her interest was now in "small p" politics.

Syndicated columnist Marianne Means described the
new Hillary:

The woman who negotiated with Congress over the details of sweeping health care reform now lunches with gossip columnists, enthuses about new drapery, snuggles up to her husband, romps with children and gives kindly interviews expressing dull thoughts. Instead of fighting entrenched special interests that can fight back, she focuses on causes with which few can quarrel. Now she encourages women to have mammograms and visits eager little schoolchildren.

In 1995, Hillary launched a weekly newspaper column of her own called "Talking it Over" and wrote a book on parenting called *It Takes a Village: and Other Lessons Children Teach Us*. The column debuted in at least 150 newspapers with chatty and personal reflections on topics such as how she rebelled against her Secret Service agents and drove herself around town during a visit to Little Rock. Other columns delve into issues such as how the president's wife can endure hours of standing in a reception line shaking hands, or how she plays hostess to a state dinner.

On the occasion of her twentieth wedding anniversary, she wrote, "Like any other couple that has been together a long time, we have worked hard and endured our share of pain to make our marriage to grow stronger and deeper. We have encouraged and motivated each other, and we've had a lot of fun, too." As evidence, Hillary recounts a late night adventure with Bill. "We grabbed our towels, left the mansion, tiptoed through the Oval Office, and snuck through some bushes in pitch black. Without anybody around, we went for a midnight swim." She concludes the piece by writing, "It was a little too cold this week to celebrate our 20th anniversary with a dip in the pool. But I think I came up with an equally romantic way to mark the day. You might be able to guess what it was. But sorry, I'm not telling."

In January 1996, the mysterious "discovery" of missing Rose firm billing records just outside the First Lady's

private office in the White House residence created a
sensation. Under subpoena by the Whitewater Independent Counsel Kenneth Starr and a Senate Committee for
two years, the records were covered with notations in
Vince Foster's handwriting and detailed Hillary's deep
involvement in Jim McDougal's Castle Grande development scam.

Almost as damaging was the Travelgate controversy,
which since its eruption on 19 May 1993, refused to go
away. Seven long-time employees of the White House
Travel Office, which makes arrangements for the press
corps traveling with the president, were fired for "mis-
management" and replaced by individuals employed by
World Wide Travel, a Little Rock travel agency. The new
office director was a twenty-five-year-old cousin of the
president named Catherine Cornelius. The firings
touched off a wave of bad publicity, causing the White
House to hand over the travel office operations to American Express. Six of the seven fired employees were offered new jobs elsewhere in the government, and the
brouhaha should have blown over.

But, it did not. Billy Dale, the former Travel Office
director was accused of embezzling sixty-eight thousand
dollars and subjected to a thirty-month legal nightmare.
Not only was he forced to run up five hundred thousand
dollars in legal fees, but his adult children were interro-
gated for hours on the sources of their income. In late
1995, Dale was acquitted by a jury in less than two hours,
instantly becoming a martyr. By this time, congressional
investigators had unearthed extensive evidence that the
firings had been premeditated and the allegations fabri-
cated in order to steer the Travel Office business to World
Wide Travel and TRM, an air charter brokerage owned
by the Clintons' Hollywood friend, Harry Thomason.

A memo, which did not come to light until after
Dale's acquittal, indicated that Hillary was the driving
force behind the Travel Office firings. David Watkins,
the White House staffer actually responsible for the fir-

ings, wrote in the fall of 1993, "We . . . knew that there
would be hell to pay if . . . we failed to take swift and
decisive action in conformity with the First Lady's wishes."
Hillary's previous denials of any involvement in the firings, coupled with the seeming viscousness of the prosecution of Billy Dale, created further doubts about the
First Lady's credibility. In early 1996, polls showed that
a large majority did not believe she was truthful about
Whitewater or Travelgate, and for the first time in history, a First Lady's negative rating exceeded her positive.

The humiliation of scandal, however, pales in comparison to the humiliation of her new role as Traditional
First Lady. Nonetheless, there is every indication that
Hillary is good at it. Throughout her life, she has shown
a remarkable ability to accept and adapt to new circumstances. She clearly understands that Americans admire
and respect First Ladies. Indeed, there is no title of higher
social status in the world, except perhaps the queen of
England.

What led Hillary to initially reject the traditional First
Lady's role, even though the motivating factor in her life
has been the pursuit of status? It is generally assumed
that Hillary the feminist needed to redefine the role so
she could pursue her professional and political interests.
But, this is the wrong answer. After all, Eleanor Roosevelt
was active in a wide variety of causes, some of them
controversial and at odds with her husband's policies.
But, she never sought to "redefine" the First Lady's role.

Hillary did so because of her relationship with her
husband. She rejected the traditional role because it is
one that is based upon a nurturing relationship with the
president. American presidents have one of the most
difficult jobs in the world. It is reassuring to the American public to know that the president can find refuge
from the world's problem in his family life. First Ladies
take care of presidents, and that is why they are so important to the public and so popular.

Hillary might have been more accepting of the traditional role if her relationship with Bill were stronger. Throughout the marriage, Hillary has sought an independent identity, a reaction to Bill's infidelities. Feminists applauded when it seemed Hillary was breaking ground for all women, but in reality, her motivation was far more parochial. In a sense, her new role was not untraditional at all. Betrayed wives have competed with, and ultimately sought revenge over, unfaithful husbands from the beginning of time.

"To the question about Hillary's role—essentially, the degree and scope of her influence and authority—there is a nagging subtext: the nature of the ties that bind the Clintons," Connie Bruck wrote in *The New Yorker* on 30 May 1994. "It seems plain that his indebtedness to her must only increase with each new allegation of sexual impropriety."

While Hillary has withstood all the allegations and humiliation, she has always tried to exploit her power over Bill. Her career demonstrates an understanding between the two. Education reform was Hillary's crusade in Arkansas; it was health care in the White House. Bill has spent his political life explaining his trust in Hillary on such important matters, but he really has had no choice. A deal had been struck many years ago. The Clintons' close friend Max Brantley, who has witnessed Hillary's humiliation over the years, told Bruck, "It's hard even for those who admire and respect and love Hillary not to believe that she made a pact with the devil."

Vice President Hillary Rodham and other Maine East High School officers. Junior year, 1964. Throughout high school, Hillary was the classic "teacher's pet."

(Courtesy of Penny Pullen)

Hillary and other candidates for Wellesley College Government President, 1968.
(Courtesy of Wellesley College Archives)

Wellesley commencement, 1969. Left to right: *Board of Trustees Chairman John Quarles, Hillary, President Ruth Adams, Sen. Ed Brooke. Before the day was out, Hillary would insult Brooke.*
(Photo by Chalue/Courtesy of Wellesley College Archives)

Bill Clinton sworn in for first term as governor, 1979.
(Photo provided by *Arkansas Democrat-Gazette*)

Hillary's triumphant 1983 return to the governor's mansion.

(Photo provided by *Arkansas Democrat-Gazette*)

The "60 Minutes" interview, Super Bowl Sunday, 1992.
(AP/Wide World Photos)

First Lady-elect takes in economic conference in Little Rock on 14 December 1992.

(AP/Wide World Photos)

Harry Thomason, his wife Linda Bloodworth-Thomason, and the Clintons in late 1992. At this time, plans were already being made to purge White House Travel Office staff and insert Arkansas cronies.

(AP/Wide World Photos)

Index

Health Insurance Association
of America (HIAA), 192,
194
Health Maintenance Organiza-
tions, 192
Health Security Express, 200-
201
Heckler, Margaret, 39
Hegert, Dick, 97
Heiden, Sherry, 23
Hendron, Kim, 74
Henry, Ann, 70, 76
Henry J. Kaiser Family Foun-
dation, 194-97
Henry, Morris, 76
Hertzberg, Hendrik, 162
HIAA. See Health Insurance
Association of America
Hill, Anita, 149, 161, 170
Hillary: Her True Story (King),
37, 65, 90
Hillary Factor, The, (Nelson), 82,
94, 97, 101
*Hillary Rodham Clinton: A First
Lady for Our Time*
(Radcliffe), 34, 42, 51,
57, 71, 93, 98
Hispanics, 23, 54
Holder, Eric, 203, 204
Holmes, Eugene, 152-63
Holt, John, *Escape from Child-
hood,* 176
Holtz, Lou, 62
Hotel and Restaurant Employ-
ees International Union,
181
House Committee on Un-
American Activities,
136
Houseman, Alan, 144, 145,
146

House Republican Conference,
40
Hubbell, Webster, 88, 116, 117,
119, 128, 129
Hughes, Jack, 86
Humphrey, Hubert, 39, 40
Hunt, Albert, 161
Hurt, Blant, 111-12
Hyde Amendment, 142
Hyde, Henry, 11

I

Ickes, Harold, 179-81
Ifill, Gwen, 209
Impeachment committee, 56-
59, 65, 150. See also
Nixon; Watergate
Impressionism, 22
Inaugural balls, 88-89, 103
Inauguration Day, 184
Income taxes, 118
Indian reservations, 171, 175,
176
Industrial policy, 189
Infidelities, 11, 54, 59, 73-
74, 95-97, 99, 113-
14, 159-62, 165, 182,
207-8, 215
Information Age, 203
Institute for American Values,
178
Insurance industry, 193
Integration, 53, 61
International Association of
Democratic Lawyers,
136
Iran-contra, 135
"Irv Kupcinet Show," 33, 37
Isaac, Rael Jean, 147-48
It Takes a Village (Clinton), vii,
212

Women, Infants and Children
(WIC), 151-52
Woodall, Partrick, 193
Wood, Kimba, 204
Woods, Henry, 111
Woods, Joseph A., Jr., 58
Woodward, Bob, *The Agenda*,
180
World Trade Center bomb-
ing, 135
World Wide Travel, 213
Wright, Betsey, 73, 100-101,
106, 109, 114, 194
Wright, Lindsey & Jennings
(law firm), 97, 101
Wynette, Tammy, 159

Y

Yale Child Study Center, 52,
55
Yale Law School, 42, 46, 47-
59, 133
*Yale Review of Law and Social
Activity*, 48-50
Yellow Dogs and Dark Horses
(Starr), 66, 81, 100, 109,
112
Young Republicans, 39

Z

Zappa, Frank, 167
Zercher, Christy, 182

We welcome comments from our readers. Feel free to write to us at the following address:

Editorial Department
Vital Issues Press
P.O. Box 53788
Lafayette, LA 70505

More Good Books from
Vital Issues Press

Circle of Death:
Clinton's Climb to the Presidency
by Richmond Odom

When President Bill Clinton was governor of Arkansas during the '70s and early '80s, the state was a hotbed of drug-smuggling and gun-running. In connection with these activities, a series of murders took place. More recently, several people closely associated with Bill Clinton have died under extremely questionable circumstances. Why have so many in Clinton's circle of power become part of this circle of death? Weigh the evidence, consider the facts, and arrive at your own conclusions.

ISBN 1-56384-089-8

The Gender Agenda:
Redefining Equality
by Dale O'Leary

All women have the right to choose motherhood as their primary vocation. Unfortunately, the radical feminists' movement poses a threat to this right—the right of women to be women. In *The Gender Agenda,* author Dale O'Leary takes a spirited look at the feminist movement, its influence on legislation, and its subsequent threat to the ideals of family, marriage, and motherhood.

ISBN 1-56384-122-3

ALSO AVAILABLE FROM VITAL ISSUES PRESS